ENDORSEMENTS

"If anyone had to limit his lifetime study of economics to one book, Lamb's effort would be a good choice. Lamb builds on a tradition going back to Henry Hazlitt's Economics in One Lesson, explaining that economics isn't the dry calculus of the balance sheet. In this lively book—no equations, a handful of graphs, and plenty of real-world anecdotes—you realize we make economic choices all the time.

Resources are scarce. The unseen consequences of our actions are often overlooked. Unintended consequences abound. "Affordable housing" programs can make housing less affordable. Schemes to raise wages can throw people out of work. The Indian government's well-intentioned scheme to cut down on fatal cobra bites resulted in more cobras. Lamb even shows that if you can't beat the lottery, you can use human behavior to better your (still bad) odds.

The world would be a better place if everyone, including our political leaders, read this book—especially our political leaders."

WILLIAM "BILL" STYRING III

Economist and former Senior Fellow, Hudson Institute

Economics is Like Sex

ECONOMICS
IS LIKE *Sex*™

Common Sense Thinking for Better Decisions Through the
Taboo Topics of Money, Budgets, Markets, and Trade.

JONATHAN M. LAMB

NEW YORK

LONDON • NASHVILLE • MELBOURNE • VANCOUVER

ECONOMICS IS LIKE *Sex*™

Common Sense Thinking for Better Decisions Through the Taboo Topics of Money, Budgets, Markets and Trade

Published in New York, New York, by Morgan James Publishing. Morgan James is a trademark of Morgan James, LLC. www.MorganJamesPublishing.com

Economics is Like Sex is a trademark of J Lamb Investments, INC.

The Morgan James Speakers Group can bring authors to your live event. For more information or to book an event visit The Morgan James Speakers Group at www.TheMorganJamesSpeakersGroup.com.

ISBN 9781683507222 paperback
ISBN 9781683507239 eBook
Library of Congress Control Number: 2017912750

Cover Design by:
Megan Whitney
megan@creativeninjadesigns.com

Interior Design by:
Chris Treccani
www.3dogcreative.net

In an effort to support local communities, raise awareness and funds, Morgan James Publishing donates a percentage of all book sales for the life of each book to Habitat for Humanity Peninsula and Greater Williamsburg.

Get involved today! Visit
www.MorganJamesBuilds.com

"It has been said that politics
is the second oldest profession.
I have learned that it bears a striking
resemblance to the first."

~ Ronald Reagan

CONTENTS

ACKNOWLEDGEMENTS

I want to thank my family, friends, teachers, coaches, professors, business associates, advisors, mentors, and of course my wonderful employees. I must give special thanks to my wife, Mollee, the love of my life and the mother of my two wonderful boys. She has been supportive in my crazy life journey and all my business adventures and so instrumental during what amounted to over a two-year commitment to write this book. Without the love and support of my wife and boys during the rollercoaster ride of life and business, I surely would have lost my mind long ago.

A special thank you to Jennifer Hanchey, Bill Johnson, Teresa van den Barselaar, David Hancock, Jim Howard, and the team at Morgan James Publishing—without them, this book would not have come to life, been edited, or wound up in the hands of those of you who want to have a better understanding of economics. A heartfelt thank you to Dr. Cecil Bohanon, professor of economics at Ball State University, a wonderful mentor and voice of encouragement who has always pushed me outside of my comfort zone. He taught me to believe that I—and anyone with a bit of economic understanding—can change the world for the better.

INTRODUCTION

Comedian Jerry Seinfeld has become one of the wealthiest celebrities in the world, with an estimated net worth of more than $870 million. He made a career out of finding and highlighting the humor in the obvious.

In one of Jerry's classic standup comedy sketches, he talks about a study he'd read about public speaking. According to this study, speaking in front of a crowd was the number one fear of the average person. Number two was death. As he so elegantly puts it: "For the average person, if you have to be at a funeral, you would rather be in the casket than giving the eulogy!"

Let's play our own game of "Would you rather?" For those of you who can conquer the fear of public speaking, would you rather give a speech on sex . . . or a speech on how much money you earned last year and your net worth?

Wow, that is a hard one. Who would want to get up in front of a crowded room and talk about how much money they make? That's because, for some of us, we think we make too much money. For others, we think we don't make enough. All of that is much more uncomfortable than talking about sex. Jerry's right. It would be more comfortable being in the casket!

It's estimated that Jerry Seinfeld made $43.5 million in 2016. If he was a working stiff, punching a timeclock 40 hours a week, he would be bringing home $20,913.46 per hour. That's $348.56 per minute or $5.81 per second. Not too bad. Yet, for all that money, I have a feeling that Seinfeld himself wouldn't be very comfortable talking to a group of Indiana factory workers fighting to keep their families fed about how much he earns. Equally, it would be just as hard for those same factory workers to stand up at their 20-year class reunion and tell everyone how much money they made last year.

I know, because I've been on both sides of that money speech, and that's why I've written this book. I hope to give you insights into the world of economics as it relates to the taboo topics of money, budgets, markets, and trade. With these nuggets, you'll have the confidence to talk about any of it, to anyone, regardless of the setting.

I have undergraduate degrees in economics, risk management, and insurance. I went on to pursue a master's and PhD in economics, only to drop out to start the first of seven businesses I now have under my belt, before coming full circle to return to the classroom to earn my MBA.

After earning my undergraduate degrees, I became a commodities trader, working on a trading floor and managing an electricity trading book of business with billions of dollars in assets.

I've started seven businesses, had a few that didn't turn out as planned, a few that were extremely successful, and I am still running and building two of them, either of which could become the next wildly successful, world-changing company or fizzle out and never turn a profit.

I've invested my entire life savings and retirement funds in ventures, only to lose it all. But I have other investments that have paid off, and like other entrepreneurs, I hope my current companies will pay off in the future and earn all that lost capital back and then some.

The journey of entrepreneurship is filled with the highest of highs and the lowest of lows. I've been in both camps more times than I care to remember. And I wouldn't have it any other way.

I've not had a "real" paycheck since 2012. As a business owner and consultant, I've gone months, sometimes even years, without earning any income. I've spent thousands of hours and dollars researching and writing this book, had business ventures come and go, and overseen commercial real estate deals that took, and will take, years to produce any profits.

Not many people understand what it's like to work for "free" or, worse yet, to "pay" to work. Fellow entrepreneurs, we not only don't earn a paycheck, but we often lose money. Talk about a hard pill to swallow! Some days, it actually costs us money to get out of bed.

Yet through it all I've learned how to do more with less, and I've learned what true happiness means to me and my family. (I know this is true for many other entrepreneurs as well.)

My public speech about how much money I earn—or my lack thereof—may be more uncomfortable than that of most, but I'm proud of my story, and through my success and failures I've learned much on this journey of life.

Taboo

It's an unfortunate reality that money and sex are two completely taboo topics in American society. No one wants to talk about either—at least not in respectable circles. Parents leave both topics to the schools to deal with. But even then, students spend just a semester of their physical education class learning about "reproduction" and another semester of their social studies curriculum on "economics." The result is that we produce generation after generation of people who are improperly educated on two of the most important subjects in our lives.

My oldest son has been inquisitive since he learned to talk and has a million questions about everything. He's gone up to countless people and asked how much their shoes cost. Or he might say, "That's a really nice car! How much money do you make?"

Few adults would do that. It's just not done in our society. You may as well ask a woman how old she is and how much she weighs. The problem with this approach, however, is how can we learn if we don't ask questions?

Our shying away from open discussion about sex and money has resulted in many misconceptions. Because people truly don't understand either topic, they avoid talking about—and even thinking about—these matters altogether. As a result, people are "educated" via dirty jokes, the Internet, and cable TV.

Hollywood and the media have been teaching generations of kids that money is happiness. In the next breath, they portray money as something evil, proof of corruption on Wall Street, or the handiwork of supervillains. Because of this, far too many people think Wall Street is run by people who lie, cheat, and steal.

People go on to connect money with economics. Because most are taught about economics in social studies and the only people who talk about economics are politicians, people relate the subject to something that only concerns government. And guess what? Thanks to Hollywood and the media, we're led to believe that all politicians lie, cheat, and steal. Once again, money is vilified and good, hardworking, honest people hide their successes (or failures).

It's time this situation changes. Money is not inherently bad. Sex is not inherently bad. We should not be embarrassed by either. We should be open to talking about both. And that's why I've written this book. I'm going to free you of the shackles slapped on you since you learned to talk.

For you to truly understand sex and money, we must go all the way back to the beginning of time. I'm sure you've heard that prostitution is the oldest profession. Ronald Reagan would have you believe politics isn't much younger. Both beliefs are wrong. Economics wins the title of the oldest profession.

Unfortunately, society often views economists with the same contempt as it does prostitutes, politicians, used car salesmen, and weather forecasters. Economics gets a bad rap, yet it's the most important thing in our lives. Whether or not you recognize it, economics is constantly in motion. Everything has a cost: goods, services, money, and time. Economics is simply cause and effect and the understanding of costs and tradeoffs.

Long before streetwalkers and smooth talkers, there were basic economic principles driving their career choices. Before entering either profession, prostitutes and politicians had to answer the same questions:

- What are the costs of my profession?
- What price should I charge?
- How much would it cost me to run for president or become a high-end escort?
- What are the benefits of embarking on this career?
- Is prostitution the most profitable industry for me, or would I be better suited to politics?

Come to think of it, every conceivable profession is judged using similar questions. Economics isn't a boring subject filled with charts and theories cooked up by some dead guys who lived centuries ago. Instead, economics is about decisions, decisions that relate to money, life, love, and happiness. Economics is a social science that analyzes and predicts people's actions based on incentives. And it's omnipresent. Every decision you make, every action you take, rests on economic principles.

So let's put one horrible misconception to rest before we embark on this journey of financial and sexual enlightenment (if you will): economics isn't just about government policies, interest rates, unemployment, and other topics that make for literary sleeping pills. No, economists analyze a vast array of topics you'd never consider, ranging from love and war to crime and courtrooms; from sports and drugs to advertising and couponing; from casinos to digital downloads. And, yes, there's even the economics of sex, dating, and marriage. If you can identify with some commonsense principles, you can understand the world of economics.

Think of it this way: economics is a lot like sex. Everyone's an expert, yet nobody really understands its true complexities. Well, this book will help unravel some of the mysteries so you'll have a better understanding of your world, your actions, and your decisions. As a result, you'll find more rewarding social, business, and financial opportunities.

CHAPTER 1

WE CAN'T HAVE IT ALL

've had the privilege of learning from many successes and failures in my life. I spent over eight years on two different trading floors, running books of businesses with billions of dollars in assets. I've also started many different businesses, developed commercial real estate, owned franchises, and owned a consulting business where I financed millions of dollars of projects for a host of customers across an array of businesses.

One of the seven businesses I owned was a small home remodeling company with about 25 employees. We made it a point to educate our staff and customers:

If you want it GOOD and FAST, it won't be CHEAP.
If you want it GOOD and CHEAP, it won't be FAST.
If you want it FAST and CHEAP, it won't be GOOD.

When deciding on home remodeling or any other purchase, you get to choose among good, fast, and cheap. You can have any two of the three, but you can't have them all. There's always a tradeoff. And *that* is one of the fundamental ideas behind economics.

Economics is the study of production, distribution, and consumption of goods and services. In other words, for any nation (and individual), we must figure out what to produce, how to distribute it, and who's going to get it.

Do we want to use our land for farming, or should we plow our corn under and build a baseball field like Kevin Costner? Should we grow corn for food or fuel? Should we chop down trees to make expensive homes or cheap pencils? Should college students major in marketing, math, or medicine? We must answer these and countless other complex questions because of one simple reason: "You can't have your cake and eat it too." We can't have it all.

While we do have an abundance of resources—land, labor, and capital—they're not unlimited. We can only create so many goods and services each year, so we must make decisions on what should get produced. Because resources are limited, every decision results in a tradeoff, a cost.

Is there a cost for reading this book? Aside from the price you paid for it, you'd most likely answer no. For anyone who received this book as a gift, checked it out of a library, or illegally downloaded it from the Internet, he'll absolutely answer no. We economists see it differently; we don't see costs as only dollars and cents. Instead, we view costs as the highest valued thing given up in exchange. If you spend one hour reading this book, you lost an hour in which you could have been working, shopping, watching a movie, or searching for a one-night stand. The lost event you value the most is the cost of that hour.

If your boss offered you $50 per hour for overtime but instead you spent your time reading this book, then it cost you $50 an hour. You indirectly gave up $50 in exchange for reading this book. That's every bit as much of a cost as if you pulled out a $50 bill from your wallet. Economists call this *opportunity costs* since it reflects a lost opportunity. And there is *always* a cost for every action. Maybe your grandfather taught you, as mine taught me, "There's no such thing as a free lunch." Nothing is free—even if you're not necessarily forking out cash or swiping the plastic.

For example, if the United States decides to make more pencils, we must have less paper because we make both from a limited resource: trees. If we use that wood for pencils, we can't also use it to make paper. So the cost of pencils is paper. We can't have it all. If we choose pencils, we sacrifice paper. If we use steel to make cars, we must produce fewer bridges. The cost of cars is bridges. For every bikini model, there's one less lingerie model. All of this is because resources are limited, while our wants are limitless.

There are only so many trees growing, and they grow at differing speeds. Replenishing the supply takes time. There's only so much steel being produced for only so many hours in the day. No matter what you decide to do, whether it's working or relaxing at the beach, there's a cost because we can't have it all. At a bare minimum, there's a cost of time. You can't use the time you spend doing one thing to do something else. Unless, of course, you have a DeLorean with a flux capacitor.

Here's a trickier problem: let's say you're walking down the road and spot a rogue apple tree. You pick an apple and eat it. Isn't that free? Nobody paid for the apple. Nobody planted the seed that became the apple tree. You were walking anyway, so your time wouldn't have been used for something else. All true, but that apple was a resource that can no longer be used. You ate it, so the world has a little less apple pie.

No matter how hard you try to find something in life that's free, you'll fail. There is always a cost. There is no free lunch. It's because non-economists fail to understand this simple fact that their judgments on government rules and regulations are flawed. People make arguments over benefits but completely neglect the costs. It's easy to do if you're looking for costs as dollars and cents, and it's always easy to overlook what you can't see.

Hoodlums, Bricks, and Windows

In 1850, French economist Frédéric Bastiat wrote an insightful essay titled "What Is Seen and What Is Unseen." He used a parable of a broken window to prove why destruction doesn't create a net benefit to society. It highlights the dangers of overlooking opportunity costs.

There's nothing I like more than a new suit, and a modern version of that parable tells of a tailor who makes men's suits. One day he arrives at work to find his storefront window shattered. The offending brick—hurled by a hoodlum in the dark of the night—is laying in the middle of his shop surrounded by shards of glass. The tailor calls a glassmaker, who arrives with a fresh pane of glass and begins installing it. When it's done, the tailor pays him $300 for his services.

An observant onlooker says to the others, "Hey, this isn't so bad after all. We're seeing the glassmaker at work. He just got $300, which he'll use to buy things from others. Those people, in turn, will buy more things from others. That money would have just been sitting in the cash register, but now it's being pumped into our local economy. The glassmaker may buy new shoes, and the shoemaker may buy a new hat. We're benefitting from the destruction!"

But there's a big mistake in this reasoning. It's easy to miss the mistake if you're not counting opportunity costs. While the tailor does spend $300 to repair the window, it may be the $300 he had planned to use to buy wool to make a new suit instead. The wool seller loses $300 while the glassmaker gains $300, so there's no net benefit.

The cost of the window was a new suit. After the window is repaired, the tailor has a window but no new suit. Had the window not been broken, he'd have his original window plus a suit. But because the new suit never came into existence, it's overlooked.

We can't focus on the one person or group that benefits while completely ignoring the person or group that loses. The idea of economic thought is to understand the best way to advance society. We're better off with more goods and services, not the same or fewer.

Once you understand the fallacy of destruction, you'll find it in various forms. You'll see newspaper articles explaining why Florida's economy benefits from hurricanes, why the United States benefits from war, and why we shouldn't let our jobs be transferred overseas.

I personally have had to live through this very issue. My wife and I owned a childcare business for roughly eight years. We had about 35 employees and almost 200 children in our building at any given time.

In February 2013, one of the teachers called the front office to complain that the heat was not working. When the HVAC company arrived to fix the problem, the technician discovered that two of the units had been stolen. The thief made off with about $150 worth of copper, and the HVAC company got to sell us $20,200 worth of new HVAC units. Luckily, we had insurance, but we had to pay a $1,000 deductible, and our claim was further lowered by $3,030 due to depreciation.

Remember, "There is no such thing as a free lunch." The HVAC company was $20,200 happier, but we had $4,030 less money in our bank account to give teachers raises or buy new supplies, and the insurance company had $16,170 less in its bank account to give its employees raises or return to shareholders. Extend the argument to a large scale and you'll see there's no net economic benefit from war either.

What about lost jobs? That's a hot topic and has even encouraged Walmart and other businesses to launch "Buy American" campaigns. Non-economists believe that we're better off if we keep all the money here, in the United States. Why pay someone to produce goods in Europe when we have unemployed people here? That's a great argument if you focus only on the benefits, but consider the costs and a new picture emerges.

Let's look at the benefit of free trade (i.e., the freedom to trade). Let's say the United States can produce a certain quality car for $50,000. Europe builds it for $30,000. If we encourage citizens to buy only American goods, US car manufacturers do benefit—just like the glassmaker or the HVAC company in my illustrations. However, all car buyers lose $20,000.

Had they not been coerced into buying only US goods and paying $50,000 for a car, they could have paid $30,000 for an imported car and had $20,000 left over to buy a boat. US boat manufacturers actually lose. Therefore, a "Buy American Cars" campaign is equivalent to launching a "Don't Buy American Boats" campaign.

One issue to note about free trade is that it doesn't equal "fair trade." In this example, we assume the European carmaker can produce cars more cheaply due to lower costs. What if the cost of that car from the European carmaker was really $70,000, but the local government had given the automaker $40,000 worth of subsidies so that the $70,000 car would only cost Americans $30,000? My point is that we must be careful to factor in the cost of subsidies because for trade to be truly beneficial to society, it must be "free" *and* "fair."

It doesn't make any sense to think it's better for society to have a relatively small group of auto-industry employees benefit when 250 million American citizens are forced to have less. The costs outweigh the benefits when you try to force people to buy only American-made goods. It's a great reminder to be circumspect and not just focus on benefits you can see. Whether it is suits, windows, HVAC units, or luxury cars, consider the costs you cannot see.

In a storybook ending, our HVAC company recommended that we install locked "cages" around our five HVAC units to protect against future theft. Insurance companies aren't in the protection business, and with our bank account $4,030 lower due to the theft, we chose not to protect the new units. Six months later, one more unit was stolen.

There is always a cost because we can't have it all. On a side note, that building now has locked cages around the HVAC units.

CHAPTER 2

IT TAKES TWO TO TANGO

ike sex, trade isn't possible with only one person. Since economics is a "complicated" way to analyze "simple" tradeoffs, economists need to look at both sides of the equation.

It may only take one person to change the world, but it takes two to tango. One person may have an idea to create a change, whether big or small, but people must respond before it works. Economists put it in simple terms: people respond to incentives. To get cooperation, you must provide proper incentives. You'll capture a dog's attention with a high-pitched whistle, but it won't do much for people. People respond better to money.

When organizing society to get the greatest value of goods and services for everyone, it helps to have a system based on incentives. When proper incentives are in place, people respond through self-motivation, without prompting from anyone. In school, it could be the incentive of a good grade. At work, it could be a raise or bonus. In relationships, it could be sex. Nobody needs to be watching and/or forcing anyone to achieve the desired outcome when the proper incentive is dangling out there.

Adam Smith, considered the father of modern economics, said that people act on self-interest. Another of his key insights is that everyone can be made better off in the process of trade, which is just a method of improving the self-interest of each side. That's the brilliance of capitalism. It may seem like we live in a nation of money-grubbing, profit-seeking people all looking to get the most for themselves, but it's that very incentive that creates all the wonderful goods and services. Capitalism works because people respond well to money. It's not a perfect system, but it's the best-known system for creating the most number of goods and services for everyone. With more to go around, more wealth is created.

In Smith's book *The Wealth of Nations*, he writes, "It is not from the benevolence of the butcher, the brewer, or the baker that we expect our dinner, but from their regard to their own interest." In other words, we don't get dinner because these people are being nice and feel like feeding everyone. Instead, it's because they can use their skills to cut steak, bake bread, and brew beer to sell for profits. Because people have an incentive to make profits, the rest of us can be assured that food will appear on our tables.

And what will these people do with their profits? They'll use them to buy things from others. The butcher can be assured he'll have knives and tables; the baker can get yeast and ovens; and the brewer can buy malt, hops, and risqué Super Bowl ads with sexy supermodels.

> " It is not from the benevolence
> of the butcher, the brewer,
> or the baker that we expect our dinner,
> but from their regard to their own interest. "
>
> ~ Adam Smith

Everyone acts to get the most money for himself, but in doing so, everyone becomes better off.

For money to be made, however, there must be a need. Nobody can force you to buy steak or bread—although during the Super Bowl, some people may feel the uncontrollable urge to buy beer, thanks to those commercials. Instead, any transaction requires that the buyer and seller feel better off after it is accomplished. *The system works because it takes two to tango.*

In sports, there's a winner and a loser, but in economics *everyone* is better off. That's the only way any transaction can happen. If the butcher buys a knife for $100, he feels the knife was worth more than the cash he forked over (pun intended). The person who sold the knife felt the cash was worth more than the knife. Both are happy. Both are better off.

The same is true in relationships. A man asks a woman out on a date, and she says yes. Though he can expect to have less money in his wallet after the date, they both think that they'll be better off going on the date than not going because there's a reward attached: company, a meal you don't pay for, a relationship, and, yes, even sex and marriage.

If there's money to be made in production, you can be assured those products will be brought to market. We have steak and beer today because people want it. We don't have steak-flavored beer because nobody wants it (yet?).

In 2016, I had an idea to start a company making custom bedsheets. It's simple: couples should have bedding that caters to each individual's tastes and preferences. We have mattresses that provide this personalization nowadays, so why not the linens?

My wife is always cold, and since I didn't want thick sheets all summer long, My Side and Yours Inc. was born. Available in a large selection of fabrics, each sheet and blanket was divided to provide an ideal sleep environment for each partner. After a lot of research, paying a boat-load of money for a patent, and setting up a supply and manufacturing chain, I launched the company.

Though the research said people loved the idea of our custom sheet sets, when it came right down to it, despite a $22 billion home-textile market size, My Side and Yours wasn't able to sell enough sheets to drive down the cost of production. And since the cost of production was high, I couldn't sell enough units to make it worth my while to keep marketing the product. After about a year in business, I closed the company.

So why are some products on the market while others are not? Because entrepreneurs are motivated by profit and will only offer products that make a profit. Products that remain on the market are there because people want those products.

But where do profits come from?

The Efficiency of Capitalism

Just as love, marriage, and sex are the results of dating, profits are the result of efficiency in capitalism. Profits result when people put their limited resources to use in the most efficient way. If you can buy sugar, flour, and eggs for a cost of $17, and the couple that just got engaged after going on their first date is willing to pay $175 for that cake to feed their wedding guests, you may be motivated to bake that cake for $158 more than the cost of the ingredients.

It's the potential for profit that ensures some of our scarce resources—sugar, eggs, flour, and time—will be put to use to produce wedding cakes. As long as people are willing to pay more than the cost of production, enterprising people will bring profitable products to market. If people were only willing to pay $17 for the cake, it would never get made because there would be no benefit to the baker. The profit motive ensures that only the products people value the most will get produced with those resources.

Non-economists often believe that profits result because someone buys something for one price and simply sticks a higher price tag on it. They feel capitalism's big fault is that everyone is forced to pay higher prices since everyone's tacking on profits, but a little thought shows that can't be true.

Notice your profit didn't result because you bought an existing cake for $17 and simply tacked on a $158 profit. Remember, you can't buy wedding cakes for $17. But you can *create* them for $17 worth of supplies plus your time. The cake came into existence because the baker took scarce resources and created something people valued more than the individual elements.

The profit motive doesn't create higher prices; it creates lower prices. Profits never accrue to those who produce things inefficiently. Why? Customers don't care about your costs. They care about price.

How would people respond if a local bakery tried to sell wedding cakes for $5,000 because it was saddled with debt, expensive property, and high salaries? They wouldn't say, "Well, it's certainly worth the price because of their high costs." Instead, that store would go out of business as everyone flocked to your store, where they can pay $175 for a wedding cake that's just as beautiful.

Capitalism ensures that only the strong survive—a tradition dating back to the prehistoric period when the strong, jock caveman, who was captain of his high school hunting team, got to take the prettiest cave-girl cheerleader back to his cave after prom. Under capitalism, only those who offer the best goods and services at the lowest prices will survive.

I'll say it again: it's the pursuit of profits that creates low prices. If another baker can produce wedding cakes more efficiently, paying only $11 in supplies and having less overhead in making the cake, he may open another bakery and offer cakes for $125. Everyone would leave your store and shop at the cheaper, yet equally beautiful, bakery next door. In response, you recognize you have lots of room for profit, so you lower your cake prices to $100.

Prices don't rise with competition. Instead, you must compete with the new seller. Eventually the price falls to a point where it's just worth somebody's time to produce that cake. It's the most efficient producer who survives. The rest of us benefit through competition.

Just like in the wedding-cake market, competition is good in dating, love, sex, and marriage. If there's one girl and 20 guys who wanted to date her, she'd be better off than if there were only two guys trying to woo her. With a choice of 20 men, she could pick the most handsome, intelligent, kind, and wealthy suitor. However, if there were only two guys who wanted to date her, she might have to settle for the poor, nerdy economist.

Now consider Walmart's "Buy American" campaign again. Does it make sense to think we're better off because Walmart is buying goods at higher US prices when it could buy them cheaper abroad? If Walmart takes this approach, another enterprising person will recognize he can compete with Walmart and build a store filled with cheaper televisions, computers, and clothes. The resulting competition would force Walmart to lower its prices and stock more foreign-made products. That's what happened when K-Mart challenged the giant. Now Amazon and other e-commerce retailers sell goods from all over the world at the click of a mouse or a swipe on a smartphone screen, and consumers, through the beauty of free and fair trade, benefit through lower prices.

Even though sex sells, believing that marketing campaigns can create prosperity by urging everyone to pay higher prices is economic nonsense.

Who Plans Our Economy?

What's really fascinating about capitalism is that no single person plans what is produced in the economy. It's a complex organization of people acting on a profit incentive. I thought it would be profitable to make custom bedsheets, and after spending tens of thousands of dollars on research, development, engineering, fabrics, manufacturing, marketing, and countless hours, I was wrong.

When opening a bakery, you need knives, but those aren't created by one person. It takes companies to mine the components that make steel, another company to produce the metal, yet another to forge it, another to create sharpening tools, another to grow trees for the wood handle, another to carve the wood, another to make rivets to fasten the handle to the blade, and so on. You also need ingredients, such as eggs and flour from farmers. But the farmers need land, tractors, seeds, barns, and of course chickens. Oh, and someone to turn that wheat into flour.

The only reason that goods and services come to market is because enterprising people recognize profits can be made. They take resources and create things of higher value. Everyone finds they have skills to create something another wants—even if it's just labor.

Just like men and women searching for the best partner, with a free capitalist society, entrepreneurs search for goods and services that bring the highest profits. There's no better incentive than happiness and profits, yet that doesn't mean they're the only ones. Incentives come in many forms, including new laws, a change in prices, or even a change in weather. No matter what the action, incentives are created, causing people to respond in certain ways. And it's only after considering incentives that you can learn to see things like an economist. Without tracing through all the possibilities, you can get unexpected—and unwanted—results.

The Law of Unintended Consequences

Those who don't understand economics often believe capitalism is inherently unfair. It seems to create a system where the rich get richer while the poor stay stuck in the trenches. That's because they focus on the idea of the profit motive, without realizing that it's the very incentive that makes others create exactly what everybody else wants. There's no perfect way to organize society, but capitalism is the best way to get the highest standard of living for the masses. Still, it's easy for people to think the government can step in and make things fair for everyone. However, when considering economic policies, you must always consider the incentives they create. Governments can create laws, but people will respond to those laws in ways that benefit them. Remember, it takes two to tango.

Without this critical thought, things can backfire, and you can get unexpected results—often the exact opposite of what was intended. Economists call these *unintended consequences.*

Seatbelts and air bags, for example, were forced into law as a way to reduce traffic fatalities. It's only logical that if you keep people safer, more lives will be saved, right? Wrong. You forgot about the incentives these products created.

I'm an old car fanatic, so I can tell you this: you don't understand the white-knuckle terror of keeping your hands on the wheel at "10 and 2" until you have driven a 1955 Pontiac Safari station wagon in rush-hour traffic with bias ply tires, no power steering, no power brakes, and no seatbelts.

When cars are safer, people drive faster. They drive closer. They're more likely to dial a cell phone, send a text, or monkey with the stereo, but it's a different story driving my old 1955 wagon. There's no technology standing between you and disaster, so you pay attention and take your time. Safer cars created riskier habits, so we now have more accidents.

While I will concede that safer cars do save more lives when they are involved in an accident, still, the number of accidents has increased, thus taking more lives. The end result is that forcing car manufacturers to install airbags and seatbelts has had almost no net effect on saving lives. Instead, pedestrian deaths increased as people found themselves walking beside riskier drivers.

So the end result—as counterintuitive as it may seem—is this: safer cars created more fatalities. It was an unintended consequence few people would have guessed. Economists did.

If You Want More Crime, Motivate!

People screamed for the government to do something to prevent violent crimes, so stricter laws were passed to make people safer. Many states enacted "three-strike" laws, which means a criminal gets life in the slammer after he commits a third violent crime. But remember, governments can create laws, but people—including criminals—will respond by doing what's best for themselves. Always ask, what incentives does this law create?

Criminals with two strikes are now more likely to kill victims or to kill arresting officers when committing their third crime. After all, life in prison is going to be the result, with or without murder, so there's a big incentive to leave no witnesses. As a result, murder rates have spiked in many of the states that passed those stricter laws—a costly unintended consequence.

How to Destroy Trees by Trying to Save Them

Recycling is a popular social campaign. At the bottom of corporate emails, in an effort to save trees, you'll often see a note that pleads with recipients not to print the communication unless absolutely necessary. Just think of all the trees that will be saved, right? Nope, that's wrong too. The recycling effort has actually reduced the number of trees and continues to do so at a steady rate.

Enterprising people have the incentive to buy land and grow trees to sell to paper mills so they can make profits. But when corporations urge society not to use paper, paper prices fall, and businesses lose the incentive to buy land to plant trees for profit. The land ends up having a higher-valued use for homes, farming, or paper recycling plants. The number of trees falls in response.

If you really want to see more trees on earth, do the opposite. Print every email. Paper prices will rise, and people will respond by purchasing property and planting tree farms. If you create profit incentives, you'll get proper responses.

More Babies with Birth Control Pills

With the introduction of each new form of birth control throughout history, birth rates have actually gone up. With increased use of oral contraceptives (the pill) starting in the 1960s and gaining widespread use in the 1970s, birth rates went up as women were less concerned about pregnancy and had more sex.

The pill had unintended consequences of not only more pregnancies but also more sexually transmitted disease as people were more promiscuous and had more unprotected sex.

How to Create Housing Shortages

For politicians, rent control is a powerful plan because it appeals to the masses and generates votes. Government rent controls were designed to keep prices low so that more people could buy houses, and as a result, we'd have fewer people living on the streets. To the untrained economics brain, it's an obvious solution. It's obvious and also wrong.

It sounds good until you consider people's reactions to the laws. With rents decreased, people lose the incentive to build apartments or to buy them as rental properties. Lower prices also give existing residents the incentive not to sell, perhaps to rent to others or to keep as a second place to live since the owner is not able to capture the full value of the property. The number of properties available for rent quickly decreases.

The lower prices, however, give the incentive for people to move to the city since rent control created "reasonable" rents. Who wouldn't want to pack up and go to the big city if you could rent a beautiful apartment for $500 per month? So people responded and moved to the cities, only to discover insufficient housing inventory. Rent controls create an effective housing shortage. If you want to find a large population of homeless people, visit any city that supports rent controls and you'll see the unintended consequences in action.

Economists aren't cold-hearted. We don't say that nothing needs to be done about the homeless. We're just saying that keeping prices artificially low for *everyone* isn't the solution. People will respond to low, rent-controlled prices in a way that forces the people who truly need affordable homes out of them.

Now it's your turn to think like an economist. What do you suppose would happen if the government created an artificially high price of some good or service? Think about the incentives to people when prices are high.

More Pollution, Please

In 1989, Mexico City recognized it had a pollution problem. The government stepped in and created Hoy No Circula, or "No Drive Day," in an effort to reduce the number of cars on the road by 20 percent. On Mondays, for instance, cars with license plates ending in five or six were not allowed to be on the road. On Tuesdays, sevens and eights were prohibited. Each day of the week was assigned two numbers that were prohibited. That ought to fix the problem, right?

Wrong. It was costly for people to be out of work for two days per week, so people responded. Rather than driving less, they bought old cars with poor emission controls—but with license plate numbers different from the ones they already owned. The number of cars on the road didn't decrease, and the amount of pollution actually increased. The law didn't solve the problem; it worsened it.

Beware of Eliminating Deadly Cobras

While Mexico had a pollution problem it was trying to fix, India had a deadlier problem. During British rule, India was infested with cobras, so the governor of Delhi devised a plan to reduce the infestation of the poisonous snakes. For every dead snake, the government paid a big bounty. The idea was that more people would hunt the snakes, and thus the snake population would decrease.

Well, sort of. People had the incentive to kill snakes, but enterprising individuals had the incentive to breed snakes to kill and sell to the government. To an economist's ear, the law made the price of snakes high, so people responded by breeding snakes. Once the government caught on, it stopped the program, but that too created an incentive. Cobra hides became instantly worthless, so the commercial breeders responded: they turned the snakes loose. The cobra laws sent more deadly snakes slithering around, not fewer. Because of this, you'll sometimes hear the *Law of Unintended Consequences* called the cobra effect.

Non-economists often believe the government can fix all problems just by creating laws. But always remember: no law has an effect until people respond. No action, incentive, or other means of enticing does any good until people respond.

Truly, it takes two to tango.

CHAPTER 3

PURSUIT OF PROFITS

Greed is good. That is, at least, the view Gordon Gekko gives in the movie *Wall Street*. In his milestone speech to the shareholders of Teldar Paper, Gekko says, "Greed, in all of its forms, greed for life, for money, for love, knowledge, has marked the upward surge of mankind."

To non-economists, however, greed is seen as an unnecessary need for material things, a desire to have more and more at the expense of everyone else. It evokes negative emotions. It's one of the seven deadly sins. It seems there's not much good that comes from greed.

But economists agree with Gordon. It may be hard to understand why economists could possibly think greed is a good idea as a way to run an economy. But let's back up and remember the point of economics: allocating scarce resources among a large population of people with unlimited wants. As soon as one need is filled, we have a need for something else.

There are always things we can think of to create, but limited resources to make them. We must make choices. What's the best way to allocate these scarce resources to get the most from them? Should we take all our gasoline and burn it to make cool bonfires for beer parties? Well, maybe, if that's the best use for it. But once a better use comes along—cars, for example—people see there's a better use, and the price of gas will rise in response.

To the untrained eye, it appears that the greedy capitalists are charging more for gasoline just because they can or just because they're trying to stick it to the little guy and keep him poor. That's simply not true. The price is rising because there's now a new need, but no additional supply.

To allocate the now relatively scarce resource, the higher price has a twofold effect: First, it makes people think twice about using gas to create bonfires. It's now expensive to do so, and people respond by doing it less often. So more gas is now available for driving cars. Second, the higher price sends a signal to the market, and the incentive for people to go find more increases. The higher the price, the greater the profits, and the more people are willing to supply gasoline.

And when that happens, the market has worked its magic and provided more gasoline, and it's all fueled by greed. Society is better off with a certain degree of greed at work. It's funny how people often see the suppliers as the greedy capitalists.

When gas prices rose sharply in 2008, everyone pointed the finger at Chevron, Exxon, BP, and other suppliers as the greedy capitalists trying to take advantage of the short supply. But, at the same time, people responded by not using boats and recreational vehicles, which conserved more of their income. They were being just as greedy. In other words, by choosing to keep more income, they elected to spend less on gasoline for lesser-valued purposes— exactly what a dictator would have done under the circumstances. This is where various economic systems differ in philosophy. While there are many different systems, you can break them down into two basic camps: those that want only a little government involvement and those that want far more—possibly all— government involvement.

Under capitalism, the factors of production—land, labor, and capital—are privately owned. Businesses and people pursue self-interest in markets, where buyers and sellers interact.

But how can people, who know nothing about running an economy, possibly be expected to know the most efficient way to allocate resources? Actually, some of the very best business people I've ever worked with, and some of the wealthiest, are successful not because they have an Ivy League education but because they understand people and what people want. This is basic, simple economics. And that's where greed is good.

Remember, people respond to incentives, and the best incentive is for people to have the ability to make a profit. When people have 100% of their own interests at stake, they have every reason to do their very best. The only way to produce a profit is to take resources from a lower-valued use and move them to one of higher value. If profit is the reward, people will find the highest-valued use for those resources. They'll produce things people truly want.

For instance, if you're a farmer, what should you grow? Will you grow crops that bring in a high price or those that bring in a low price? If tomatoes are worth $5 per bushel while onions are worth $1 per bushel, and you can grow the same bushels per acre, you'd prefer to plant tomatoes over onions, right? You'd want to maximize your well-being, so you'd choose to grow crops that can make you the most money.

The reason tomatoes bring in the most money is because they're the produce people value most, so your customers are willing to pay a high price. By looking out for your own interests, you used resources, including your labor, for their highest use. You wouldn't choose to plant asparagus that fetches 10 cents per bushel just so you could be nice and provide cheap things to the market. The low market price says that the market doesn't value asparagus highly, and it also ensures you'll use your land and skills for what society values most.

To go further, if you could make $100,000 per year as a farmer but find your land would be worth millions as a condominium, you'd choose to sell to a developer. The developer, of course, wouldn't offer that much money for the sake of being nice. He'd do it because he feels people are willing to pay that much for housing. According to the market, people value your land as a housing site more than as a farm. Naturally, things change. At a later time, people may feel a golf course would be more desirable, and you'd then see the condos torn down and replaced with 18 holes.

My grandfather and his buddy bought a farm in the late 1960s to build a golf course. Information is power, and after they purchased the land, they found out there were plans for two or three other golf courses in and around the county they lived in. In the 1960s, information like this was much harder to acquire than it is today. Reading about a proposed golf course in the daily newspaper isn't like the endless information now at our fingertips.

Instead of becoming a golf mogul, my grandfather bought equipment to farm that land. Then he bought and leased more land and eventually decided to purchase an entire International Harvester farm implement business.

Capitalism works because you have millions of people trying to figure out what something is worth. If one person has—or believes he has—a better use for a certain resource, he'll offer more money to take control of it. If it turns out to be a good choice, he'll make a profit, and society benefits.

Under communism, however, the government controls all resources and makes all decisions on what the country needs. Theoretically, all governments are trying to do the same thing. For instance, assume we abolish capitalism and make you the US dictator. How would you allocate resources? If you think the nation needs more tomatoes than onions, you'd allocate more land for tomatoes. And which land would you use? The land that looks like an awesome spot for a sporting arena or land out in the middle of nowhere that will produce tomatoes?

The answers are obvious when analyzed and explained in a book, but figuring out these areas in real-life practice is next to impossible. How can one person— no matter how good his intentions—possibly know everything about the value of all goods, services, and resources to make such important decisions? To make matters worse, you have a moving target. As peoples' values change, resource allocations must change. If people suddenly learned that onions cure cancer, how would you respond? Would you allocate 10 percent, 20 percent, or more land for growing onions?

If your head hurts thinking about it, consider that we're only talking about tomatoes and onions—two goods out of billions of things that must get produced. Any attempt to solve all the problems of resource allocation ultimately results in gross inefficiencies. Under capitalism, however, the problem is easy to solve. Just put prices on things.

Prices are one major reason the healthcare market in America is in such bad shape. Do you have any idea what a broken arm is going to cost you when you walk into your doctor's office? Unless you've had a broken arm recently or work in the doctor's billing department, it's unlikely . . . but you do know it's going to cost a small fortune.

Politicians, doctors, lobbyists, insurance companies, hospitals, and brilliant scholars can't seem to solve the healthcare crisis. Yet the solution is simple: clear, transparent prices. Both providers and patients will respond. If the price of fixing a broken arm is too high—like maybe the cost of a new car—then I won't let my boys jump on a trampoline. If the price of fixing a broken arm produces huge profits, maybe I'll go to medical school and become a doctor.

If healthcare costs are ever going to come down, prices must be transparent. Once we know prices, everyone responds to the greed incentive, and excellent allocation of resources is the outcome. There's just two questions left: How do we decide the value of things? Who sets prices?

Economists usually answer that the market sets the price. But what they really mean is that people set prices by simply searching for profits. And, remember, the only way profits appear is when people take lower-valued resources and move them to higher uses.

Farmers Set the Price of Land

In the early 1800s, economist David Ricardo devised a brilliant example to show how land values would change based on supply and demand.

Assume we have two grades of land: high and low. In the early years, when an area is forming, there's lots of land sitting vacant and very few farmers, so the value of land is quite low. As settlers begin moving in, they want to farm and naturally gravitate to the high-grade land. Landowners negotiate with the would-be farmers, but they won't get much for the land. If they try to ask too high of a price, a neighbor will likely be willing to rent out his land for less money. But over time, more farmers move in, and the supply of farmland diminishes.

Eventually, all the high-grade land will be in full use, and new farmers must move to the low-grade land.

How much should be charged for rents on the high-grade land now? It all depends on the differential in productivity. For example, let's say a farmer can farm high-grade land and produce 1,000 bushels of tomatoes per year. If tomatoes are going for $5 per bushel, the farmer can make $5,000 per year. If he pays $1,000 per year in rent, his profit is $4,000 per annum.

But once all that land is used and new farmers are forced to the low-grade land, we'll see changes in prices. Let's say the low-grade land rents for $400 per year and produces 600 bushels of tomatoes. At $5 per bushel, those farmers will make $3,000 per year. After paying the $400 rent, they'll make $2,600 rather than the $4,000 profit they'd make on high-grade land. They're worse off by $1,400, which means they should be willing to pay up to $1,400 to move to the high-grade land.

We can't change the amount of land or its productivity. But we can change price. The farmers on the low-grade land will realize they'd be better off on the high-grade land, so they will begin to offer more money to rent that land. Rents will rise and continue to increase until the two grades of land are equalized, which will happen when the high-grade land rent rises by the $1,400 differential.

Rent will eventually rise by $1,400 to $2,400 per year for the good land. Price has now made both land grades equal. Farmers on the high-grade land produce 1,000 bushels and earn $5,000, but after they pay the $2,400 rent, they earn just $2,600 per year. Farmers on the low-grade land will produce 600 bushels and earn $3,000. After the $400 rent, they're left with $2,600—exactly the same as farmers on the high-grade land.

So, was it the landowners' greed that pushed the rents on the high-grade land to $2,400? Or was it the farmers' greed to capture the difference in crop yields? Once you understand economics, you'll see that the answers are never easy. While it seems obvious to pin the blame on the landowners, they were just responding to the farmers' greed. In the end, the value of lands and crops was equalized, and all land was being used efficiently.

At any time, if the rent on the high-grade land was less than a $2,000 difference, it would pay to switch from low-grade to high-grade land. If the differential is greater, it pays to move from high-grade to low-grade. When the difference in rents is $2,000, there's no difference in the two grades of land. Price has equalized the values.

It's exactly this process that equalizes housing prices or even the differences in living standards between two cities. This is why it's not a good idea—and not quite right to say it's fair—for the government to send aid to people who, for example, lose homes by living in known hurricane, tornado, or flooding areas. After all, when they bought the homes, they knew they were cheap because of the looming risks. But once they lose their homes, everyone thinks taxpayers now have some duty to bail them out. That only makes sense if you don't consider price. The market set the price according to the risk.

What if someone tried to make a fortune by gambling in casinos but lost all his money? Should the government dig into taxpayers' pockets to bail him out? Of course not! Notice that the reverse doesn't work either. If the guy succeeded in making millions of dollars in the casino, would he think it's fair if the government took all his earnings? Obviously not. He'd fight that law to the death. He'd say he took that risk and he should keep his just rewards. Yet, if he fails to make his millions—and in fact loses money in the process—he now thinks taxpayers should bail him out.

In the same manner, if people buy cheap houses in high-risk areas, but make lots of money because they have more money to invest in other ventures, they'd never say it was fair to distribute that extra money to the taxpayers who potentially would have had to bail them out after disaster struck. What's more distressing is, citizens seem to agree with this line of thought. Certainly, citizens don't agree when considering the gambler, but when it's about housing on high-risk land, it changes their opinions.

So you now see that greed is good, and it will also help you make consistent decisions. Are you beginning to understand why economics is such a taboo topic?

CHAPTER 4

SUPPLY AND DEMAND

love cars, and I love to drive, but I hate traffic! Anyone living in a big city knows how frustrating rush-hour traffic can be. But you can use that time to learn a lot about economics.

All drivers are trying to get home as quickly as possible, so they all have the same objective: find the fastest lane. But if one driver moves to a faster lane, he now adds one more car to that lane, so the lane slows down a bit. The lane he left has one less car, so it speeds up. As all drivers compete for faster lanes, the faster lanes slow down, and the slower lanes speed up. Eventually, cars in all lanes must be moving at the same speed, as anyone who has traveled in rush-hour traffic has noticed.

In other words, there comes a time when there's no benefit to switching lanes. At that point, all lanes have equalized their speeds. You're stuck in traffic. If you're impatient like me, this is a very hard concept to accept.

A similar thing happens with free markets. Under capitalism, everyone is trying to accomplish the same thing, but rather than searching for faster lanes, they're seeking out bigger profits. They're on the hunt for opportunities where they can take scarce resources and move them to a higher-valued use. If there's a product that yields really big profits, you can be sure the producer will increase production to satisfy the demand (or new firms will enter the market and produce similar products). Either way, as production increases, buying pressure is put on the scarce resources used to make the product, and their prices rise.

At the same time, the additional supply reduces the product's price. As the resources get more expensive and the finished products sell for lower prices, profits get squeezed. Eventually, nobody has the incentive to bring more products to market—and that's when additional production stops. It's just like rush-hour traffic, in which drivers eventually have no reason to switch lanes.

As an entrepreneur, I've experienced this firsthand. In the housing boom that led to the Great Recession, granite countertops became the "must have" for new homes and kitchen remodels. Prior to the housing boom, the beautiful stone was largely imported from Italy or mined from local American quarries in places like Vermont and Minnesota. Prices for granite kitchen countertops could easily be $15,000 to $25,000.

In 2007, I bought a kitchen and bath remodeling company. (I know, great timing, right?) The company specialized in engineered stone countertops that were higher quality than slab granite. The average cost of countertops using our engineered stone was only about $5,000 to $10,000 for a full kitchen remodel.

As the world entered into recession, homeowners found that, to attract buyers, they needed to remodel their kitchens and bathrooms, but they didn't want to pay a lot. With granite reserves all over the world, American granite fabricators found that they could buy slabs from countries like India, Brazil, and China . . . and prices began to plummet. Today, depending on the color and quality of the stone, new granite kitchen countertops can be had for just a few thousand dollars, not the $15,000 to $25,000 it may have cost only a few years before, and well less than the $5,000 to $10,000 of our engineered stone tops.

Needless to say, between the sinking prices of competition and lower demand due to the downturn in the housing market, I sold our kitchen and bath remodeling company in 2013 at a very large loss, and it is no longer in business today. But does this mean there are no profits in the kitchen and bath remodeling business? Not exactly.

There must still be profits; otherwise, nobody would continue making the products. Manufacturers need enough profit to make it worth the time to continue. However, if profits get too squeezed, some companies, like mine, will drop out of the market, which causes prices to rise, making it more worthwhile for others to continue. But if profits rise too much, new entrants will appear and cause prices to fall again.

Just as with traffic, once all lanes equalize, there's no benefit to zipping into the fast lane. When markets are in equilibrium, there's no incentive for a new firm to enter the fray. Anyone new to capitalism must certainly wonder who is guiding the economy and ensuring that just enough products will be brought to market.

The answer is nobody. Our economy is guided by the collective action of everyone searching for profits. When everyone is searching for profits, somebody will find resources that can be moved to a higher-valued use. Profit is the motivation.

There's no way a centralized planning committee, such as what's used in Communist China, could ever have that type of efficiency. In fact, any economist will tell you that the Chinese economy has not, and will not, ever maximize efficiency. How could a small group of people possibly know all the goods and services needed by everyone at all times?

But when people have profit-making as an incentive, it changes things. In the words of economist Adam Smith, even though individuals are driven by profits, the overall market is led to an efficient outcome as if guided by an "invisible hand." Supply and demand allow production to equalize when there's just enough demanded by the market.

When I worked on my first trading floor out of college, the price of WTI Crude Oil was in the upper-$30-per-barrel range. It drifted up over the years until it peaked at more than $140 per barrel (this was prior to the Great Recession). I vividly remember being on the floor when a highly paid executive of our firm walked onto the trading floor and made the bold statement that "oil will never be below $100 a barrel again!" Not long after he said that, oil prices fell like a rock and then came full circle, trading in the $30s again.

It may seem like those evil "fat cats" on Wall Street or in Congress or the president or the Chinese or some James Bond villain is manipulating the prices that we pay for everything, but through learning just a bit about basic economics, you can understand how prices really work. Prices send signals through the economy as to what's needed most. If prices are high, people respond and bring those products to market.

But how are prices determined, and how did the director of Gas and Oil Trading, with a multibillion-dollar trading portfolio, get the future of oil prices so wrong?

The Laws of Supply and Demand

It's impossible to teach economics without talking about supply and demand. It helps to explain all kinds of prices and changes, including wages, interest rates, currencies, stock prices, and others.

The amount of goods and services produced in the nation depends on two things: the quantity of goods supplied and the quantity demanded by people. When we say there's a demand for a product or service, it just means people have a need or desire for it. Buyers are demanders. They respond to prices as you would expect: as price falls, people buy more; as price rises, they buy less.

This relationship is called the *Law of Demand*. While it's not a true law, like those created on Capitol Hill, it's a time-tested behavior that acts as if it were a law. Visit any store offering Black Friday super sales and you'll see people flocking to take advantage of lower prices. On the other hand, if you see prices spike higher, say when gasoline prices rise, people buy less. That's the Law of Demand in action.

Let's say a local store on a college campus finds it can sell a certain number of cases of beer per week at various prices. Notice that price and quantities move in the opposite direction: as price rises, the amount of beer people are willing to buy decreases and vice versa; this is called an inverse relationship:

Price	Number of Cases of Beer People are Willing to Buy (per week)
$10	300
$15	250
$20	200
$25	150
$30	100

Whenever we look at supply or demand, we must assume a fixed time period, such as one week, one month, or one year. Without a time reference, we can't determine an answer. How many cases of beer would you buy if beer were to cost $10? You may buy one per week, or four per month, or 48 per year. The answer depends on time.

Economists like to look at supply and demand graphically, which makes it easy to visualize what the market price should be and what will happen if prices are artificially raised or lowered. They always put price on the vertical axis and the amounts (quantities), or sales, on the horizontal axis. By putting the numbers from the above table on a graph, we get the following picture:

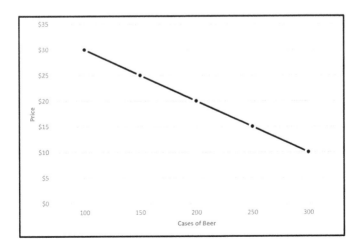

The demand line is downward sloping, meaning it begins in the upper left corner of the chart and gradually falls toward the lower right corner. This is a direct result of the Law of Demand. Notice that as price falls, more beer is sold. So the road to big profits may sound easy: just keep lowering your prices, and sales will rise. Only, the solution isn't that easy. Buyers are only part of the economy. We need to understand what motivates sellers.

The Law of Supply

Buyers can't buy anything unless someone is willing to sell. Sellers respond in the opposite way to buyers: as prices rise, sellers are willing to sell more, and as prices fall, they're less motivated and will decide to sell less. This relationship is the *Law of Supply*, which is just the opposite of the Law of Demand. If market prices begin rising, sellers become more motivated and will increase staff, equipment, or other factors to capture the high prices. As prices fall, they're less motivated and will decide not to sell as much.

Sellers are also part of the economy. They respond to prices just as buyers do, but in the opposite direction. Sellers like high prices. Let's say the store owner is willing to sell a particular number of cases of beer per week for particular prices. Notice as the price rises, the seller is more motivated and encouraged to sell more:

Price	Amount Willing to Sell (per week)
$10	100
$15	150
$20	200
$25	250
$30	300

By plotting the above numbers on a chart, we get the following picture:

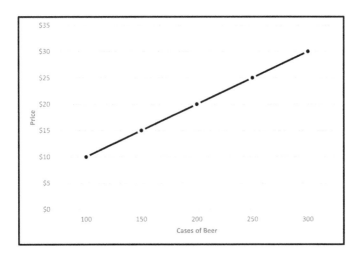

The supply line is opposite of the demand curve, so it's upward sloping. It begins in the lower left corner of the chart and gradually rises to the upper right corner. This is a direct result of the Law of Supply. As the price rises, more beer is sold.

So what's the big deal with a supply and demand chart? Well, the Law of Demand and Law of Supply provide tremendous insights into the inner workings of an economy. They shed light on many misconceptions and illusions. They help you to think like an economist and see why many of today's policies are going to leave us worse off. All you need to do to see this clearly is overlay the supply and demand lines on the same graph as shown:

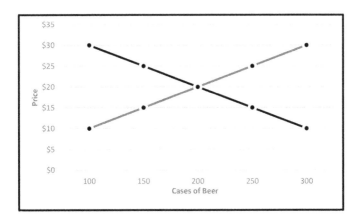

Because the supply and demand lines move in opposite directions, there must be a point where they cross. In the above chart, it's where the lines forming the "X" intersect. At that point, the amount supplied is exactly the same as the amount demanded, and as Indiana Jones so eloquently pointed out in *The Last Crusade*, "X marks the spot!" Put simply, it's where supply equals demand.

When supply equals demand, everybody who wants to buy or sell at the price can do so. There are no shortages or surpluses. We don't have excess inventory sitting on the shelves, and we don't have willing buyers who can't purchase because everything is sold out. In economics lingo, we say the market has cleared and is in equilibrium.

In the next chart, it's easy to see the market clearing price is $20, which means 200 cases of beer are sold per week:

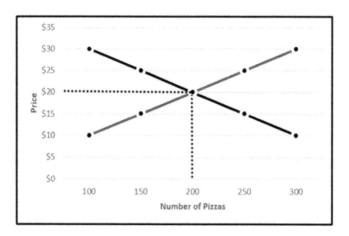

The *market clearing price* is the price we should see in the market. The store should charge $20 per case of beer and be content to sell 200 cases per week. But why should the price be $20 when some people are willing to pay more? Or why shouldn't the price be less so sales can be increased? Business owners have a powerful incentive to find the market clearing price for one simple reason:

The market clearing price is the point at which the seller's revenues are maximized.

There's no other price that the store owner can charge that puts more money in his pocket. The table shows that revenues are maximized at $20:

Price	Amount Willing to Buy (per week)	Amount Willing to Sell (per week)	Revenues
$10	300	100	$1,000
$15	250	150	$2,250
$20	**200**	**200**	**$4,000**
$25	150	250	$3,750
$30	100	300	$3,000

To understand why, remember that if the store owner sells cases of beer for $10 each, patrons may be *willing* to buy 300, but he's only *willing* to sell 100. People respond to incentives, and the store owner's supply curve showed he'd only be motivated to sell 100 cases of beer if the price was $10. Sure, lots of people may be willing to buy a case of beer for $10, but there won't be enough to go around for everyone who wants to buy at that price. Therefore, only 100 cases will be produced and sold at $10 for a total revenue of $1,000 per week.

At a price of $15, people are willing to buy 250 cases of beer, but the store owner is only willing to sell 150, so that's what he does, bringing in just $2,250 revenue per week.

At $20, the owner is willing to sell 200 cases, and people are also willing to buy 200 cases. The market is cleared. Everyone who wishes to buy at that price can do so. The store now brings in $4,000 per week, but would the owner earn more by charging a higher price?

At $25, the store owner is quite motivated to sell 250 cases of beer; however, he'll only manage to sell 150 per week, for a total revenue of $3,740. That's because people are only willing to buy 150 cases at that price. The store owner will figure this out and only inventory 150 cases, even though he's willing to sell more. The market simply doesn't demand 250 cases of beer at $25 each. His revenue has fallen from $4,000, so he's better off dropping his price to $20.

And, finally, at a price of $30 per case of beer, the owner is extremely motivated and willing to sell 300 cases per week. But at such a high price, the market is only willing to buy 100. The store's revenue falls to $3,000 per week—

significantly less than $4,000—even though the owner is charging a higher price. Again, the seller has the incentive to drop his price to $20.

The very best any business can do is to charge a price where the amount it's willing to supply is exactly matched with the amount people are willing to buy— the point where supply equals demand.

The Three Little Bears: Too High, Too Low, and Just Right

The supply and demand graph shows what happens if the store owner charges any price other than $20 per case of beers. At any higher price, the amount supplied and demanded isn't equal.

At a price of $25 per case, for example, the following chart shows the store is willing to sell 250 cases, but people are only willing to buy 150 total cases. The supply of beer would be far greater than that demanded, and the price will fall, as shown by the arrow, thus pushing the price toward the $20 crossing point.

When price is greater than the equilibrium price, there will be a surplus, which creates downward pressure on price.

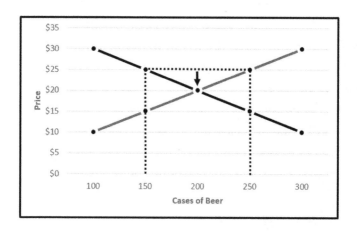

The opposite occurs for any price below the market clearing level. For instance, look at the following chart and notice that, for any price below the $20 market clearing point, supply and demand will again not be equal.

At a price of $15, the store is willing to supply 150 cases, but people are willing to buy 250 cases of beer. The demand is greater than the supply, so there will be upward pressure on price toward the $20 market clearing price.

When price is less than the equilibrium, there will be a shortage, which creates upward pressure on price.

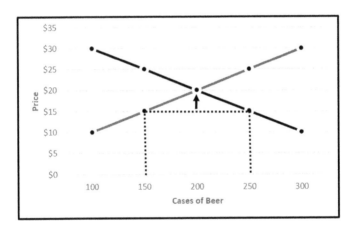

The important point to understand is that if supply is greater than demand, price will be driven lower. On the other hand, if demand is greater than supply, price will be driven higher. The greater the disparity between the price and market clearing point, the greater the pressure on price. Only when the price is $20 will there be no pressure for price to rise or fall.

Once you understand supply and demand, you can see why it's a fallacy to think capitalism exploits consumers by allowing business owners to simply charge higher and higher prices. While sellers are certainly free to set prices, they must always work within the constraints of the market demand.

As price rises, people buy less, and the business must take that into account. If people aren't willing to pay the price, nothing will be sold, so business owners have powerful incentives to charge the market clearing price—not a penny more or less.

Changing Supply and Demand

In the real world, supply and demand are never constant. They're always changing. Perhaps a new competitor enters the market so that more goods and services are now being supplied. Maybe a new product makes an old one less desirable, so the amount people want is reduced.

As supply and demand change, price will change. Changing prices is simply a reflection of changing supply and demand. What happens to price if the supply or demand changes?

Let's start with a change in supply. If more supply is brought to market, economists say there's an increase in supply. Perhaps the store owner finds that another store opens across the street. Now there are two stores providing beer to the same limited area. How can both stores sell to the same number of people? Price must fall.

The same thing happened in the oil market after prices peaked in 2008. Oil producers saw that it was profitable to pump more oil, and by drilling more wells and using fracking and other new technologies, they simply pumped more oil. Graphically, economists show this as a shift in the supply curve. Going back to the upward sloping supply graph, if supply is increased, it means there's more supply at every single price.

In the chart below, 150 cases of beer per week were supplied at $15. But if supply is increased, it means more than 150 cases of beer are now being supplied at that same price.

Whether it's the same store deciding to sell more or a new store that opens nearby, people are now willing to sell more beer at that price. Maybe they'll sell 200 cases at $15. This means the point at $15 must no longer line up at 150; it must move to the right and line up with 200, as shown below.

But it's not just the point at $15 that moves. No matter what the price is, there are now more people willing to sell more cases of beer. Every point on the supply curve shifts to the right, as you can see in the chart below:

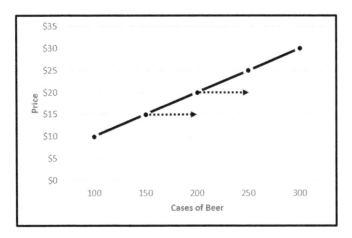

What effect does this have on the market clearing price? Price will be driven lower, which is evident once you see the supply curve shift on a supply and demand graph.

In the next chart, notice that the original market price was $20 with 200 cases of beer sold per week (shown by the shaded dotted line). But with an increase in supply, the curve shifts lower and to the right. The new equilibrium price is driven lower, to $15. Because of the lower price, people are willing to buy more, so the cases of beer sold rises to 250.

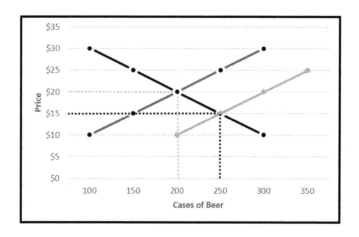

When supply increases, price falls and the quantity demanded increases.

It's a technical point, but it's important to understand that you should not say the demand increased, even though the cases of beer rose from 200 to 250 cases per week. The demand didn't increase. Instead, the supply increased, and that caused the price to fall. People responded to the lower prices and bought more beer. The only time we say the demand increases (or decreases) is if the *demand* curve shifts. We'll talk about this in a moment.

Naturally, if the supply is decreased, we'd get the opposite effect. The price would rise, and the amount that people desire would fall. Rather than the supply curve shifting to the right, it would shift upward and to the left, as shown:

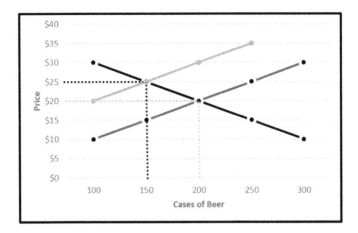

If supply decreases, price will rise. In response to the higher price, people buy less beer. The new equilibrium price is $25 with 150 cases sold each week.

When supply decreases, price increases, and the quantity demanded falls.

You'll often hear that we're in danger of running out of oil, but because of price, it'll never happen. If oil supplies continue to fall, the price will continue to rise. Even if we're down to our last gallon, it won't be priced so that someone can buy it to drive to the office. Instead, the price will be outrageously high—perhaps millions of dollars per drop—thus only allowing uses for high-end research.

The high price will give everyone the incentive to quit using oil. It'll also give the incentive for others to search for additional supply or develop alternatives. In fact, if there's anything good that comes out of higher oil prices, it's that others have the incentive to come up with alternative uses to increase the supply. If the supply is increased, prices will fall. However, if oil is super cheap, there's no incentive for anybody to go out and find even cheaper alternatives.

Remember, changes in supply alter people's perceptions about what it's worth. If there are only a few of the goods available but a high demand for them, you can be sure the price will rise. The higher price means people will buy less.

If supply is great, people won't see much value in it, so price will fall. The lower price means people will buy more, so the quantity demanded will rise.

Shifts in Demand

Changes in demand work in a similar way to shifts in supply. The only difference is that we're shifting the demand curve, and for different reasons.

If people suddenly desire more of a certain product, we say there's an increase in demand. With a higher desire for the product, people are willing to pay more. Changes in demand usually arise from changes in tastes and preferences, in income, price of related goods, consumers' expectations, or the number of buyers in the market.

With our beer example, remember sex sells, and maybe a national campaign filled with bikini-clad supermodels tells the public that beer is the fountain of youth. Or maybe a new apartment complex opens on campus, increasing the number of students there. With more students on campus every weekend, they'll desire and demand more cases of beer per week. An increase in demand means that, at *all* prices, people now desire more beer. The demand curve shifts upward and to the right, as shown in the following chart:

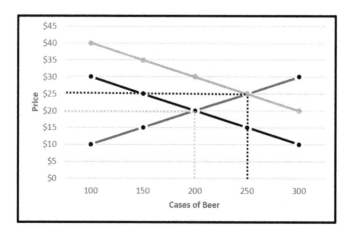

The original equilibrium price was $20 with 200 cases sold (shown by the shaded dotted line). With the higher demand, people are now willing to buy more beer at the same price. But because there aren't more cases of beer available, price will rise. The new equilibrium price becomes $25 with 250 cases of beer sold per week.

When demand increases, price rises and the quantity demanded increases.

Demand can rise, but it can also fall. Let's assume a negative government report comes out, and instead of using bikini-clad supermodels, the ads feature shirtless, overweight old men with no front teeth talking about the health risks of drinking beer. The government's anti-beer, anti-sex campaign is going to change people's tastes and preferences away from beer. People begin to reduce the amount they drink per week, and the price falls.

In the chart below, the new equilibrium price falls from the original equilibrium of $20 and 200 cases sold per week to $15 and 150 cases sold per week.

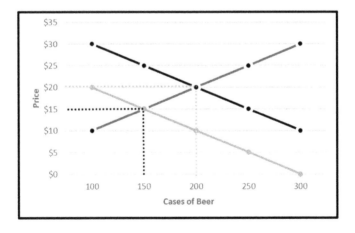

When demand decreases, price falls and the quantity demanded decreases.

When demand falls, store owners recognize they aren't selling the usual amounts. So they begin to reduce the supply to match the amount desired by people. If people only want 150 cases of beer per week, why must the price fall? Remember, the equilibrium price is where sellers will maximize their profits, so they have a big incentive to find this price. The price will fall to match the lower demand.

Prices come in various forms: price, interest rate, wage rate, currency exchange rate, and many others. Despite all the fallacies surrounding price and the reasons these numbers may rise or fall, it's strictly due to one reason: prices fluctuate to match the amount supplied and the amount demanded.

When you see that gasoline prices spiked overnight, it's not because oil producing nations decided to arbitrarily increase price, as is often believed. If it's an overnight spike, the reason is likely a sudden supply disruption, such as an attack on an oil rig or an outage at a refinery.

If there's instantly less oil, but the world still needs a certain amount, the only thing to do to address the shortage is to raise the price. No person, business, or country has the incentive to artificially raise prices because, just like in our traffic example, in the long run market prices create the greatest profit.

Capitalism Creates Competition and Employment

Because of capitalism, if there's a big demand for a good or service, many suppliers show up to capture the profits. As more suppliers enter the market, prices are driven lower, which benefits everyone (of course buyers benefit from lower prices, but even sellers can benefit from lower prices when more sales create higher profits). It's the presence of other sellers that keeps competitors from charging too much. If the price of one product gets too high, people will switch to a competitor.

For instance, assume our store owner discovers there's a bigger-than-expected demand for beer. He began by selling cases of beer for $20, but consistently finds there's a long line of people, and he can't sell beer fast enough to satisfy the demand, so he ends up turning away customers.

Being the capitalist and entrepreneur that he is, to capture bigger profits, he'll raise prices. His new, higher prices cause fewer people to buy beer, which equalizes the market. At the higher price, everyone who wants to buy beer at that price will do so, he will maximize profits, and he'll no longer turn away customers.

Of course, the store owner may also choose to increase production, but he'll have to hire more employees, buy more refrigerators, keep longer hours, or maybe even open a new store. That, of course, takes time. In the short run, he'll simply raise prices.

As the price rises, however, others will notice the big potential profits. If the store owner doesn't increase inventory, you can be sure someone else will. But it's all because of the rising price that people respond and enter the market. It's because of the excess demand that jobs are created and prices fall. Lower prices make everyone better off.

The chart below shows the original equilibrium at $20 with 200 cases of beer sold each week:

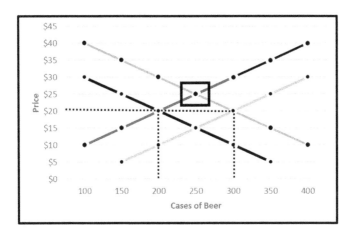

The increased demand pushed the demand curve upward to the right at a temporary equilibrium of $25 and 250 cases sold per week (shown by the square). After the store owner increases his selection and inventory, or as new businesses enter the market, the supply curve shifts downward to the right and creates a new equilibrium of $20 and 300 cases supplied each week. Because of prices and the pursuit of profits, the market brought exactly the amount of beer the people demanded.

Connecting the Dots: Price versus Value

Warren Buffett once said, "Price is what you pay. Value is what you get." Or maybe your grandfather told you, like mine told me, "You get what you pay for."

Economists agree.

We all know what price is: it's the amount you see on the price tag. But isn't value the same thing? Not at all. Value is the perceived benefit you receive.

To solve many economics problems, you must realize the difference between price and value. It's a subtle distinction, but one that allows us to make sense of how people will respond to certain incentives. People respond to incentives, but the incentives change as supply and demand change.

Economists take the idea of value a step further and recognize the value to the user is really the "next use" of that product or service. Economists call the next use of something the *marginal value*. The word marginal just means "additional" use of something.

For example, let's say you're thirsty and willing to pay $5 for a single beer. That's your perceived value. You find a bar that sells it for only $1. Because the price is below the value to you, you decide to buy it. After drinking it, however, you're not quite as thirsty as before, so the next beer won't have as much value to you. You may only value a second beer at $3, so it's still worth it to pay $1. Each beer makes you a little less thirsty (and a little more drunk), so the value of each additional beer declines.

You may be willing to pay 75 cents for a third beer, but because the price is $1, you decide to stop drinking. Even though price remained at $1, your decision to continue drinking changed because your perception of value changed. It was the relationship between price and value for the third beer that drove your decision to stop.

Notice that the marginal value declined, but the total value increased. The value to you was $5 for the first beer, $3 for the second, and 75 cents for the third, for a total value of $8.75. But three beers would have only cost $3, so why not buy it? The reason is that the third beer wasn't worth that much to you. That's what determined your action to stop.

The idea to understand is that as the supply of anything increases (more beer purchased in this example), the value declines. Eventually, a point is reached where the price will be greater than the value, and that's when people stop buying.

I will never forget the time when I called a buddy of mine around noon, and when he answered he sounded terrible. Unbeknownst to me, he was three hours behind in Las Vegas, and I had woken him up. He told me that the night before he had lost about $100 at the card tables, but drank about $300 worth of complementary beer, and now he wished he had instead lost $300 and drunk $100 worth of beer!

What's a Bag of Grain Worth?

Austrian economist Eugen Böhm von Bawerk makes marginal value clear with an interesting example: a farmer with five bags of grain. He uses the first bag to make bread to survive. The second he uses to make more bread that he can eat to be strong enough to work. The third will feed his farm animals. He'll use the fourth to make whiskey, and he'll feed pigeons with the fifth.

Notice that as the supply of grain increases (number of bags), the farmer assigns lower values to them (this holds unless, of course, he's in college and would place a higher use on grain to make whiskey).

That's partly the Law of Supply: the more of one thing you have, the less value each additional unit provides. In economics, it's called *diminishing returns*. While you gain more total satisfaction, the additional satisfaction gets reduced.

How will that farmer react if one bag of grain is stolen in the night by the thief who took my HVAC units at our daycare business? Think about it for a moment. What would you do? The answer is important for solving many economics problems.

People seek to maximize profits, which means they'll also minimize losses. To minimize his losses, the farmer won't reduce each of the above uses by one-fifth. It wouldn't make sense to stop eating, making bread, or feeding farm animals just because one bag is missing. That would be a high price to pay.

Instead, the farmer stops feeding the pigeons. It's the use he assigned to the last bag, the marginal bag, that determines his actions. If another bag is stolen, he won't make whiskey. As the supply of his grain gets smaller, the use of the next bag, the marginal use, increases. If he's down to his last bag of grain, the price gets higher: his life depends on it.

So what's a bag of grain worth? It depends on how many bags you have and what values you assign to them. Marginal values explain apparent paradoxes in capitalism, like the diamond-water paradox: why are diamonds more expensive than water when water is essential to life?

The answer is that water has a tremendous amount of total value; without it, we would die. But because there is so much water available, your next use of water is probably not going to be used to save your life. Instead, your next use of water is like the fifth bag of grain for the farmer. It will probably have a low-valued use, perhaps to wash your hands or water your lawn.

Diamonds, on the other hand, are in short supply, so your next use of a diamond is not going to be for some trivial use. The next use of a diamond has more value than your next use of water, so the marginal value of diamonds is greater than that of water. That's why diamonds cost more.

Of course, if the supply of water dried up to where you were down to your last drop and on the verge of death, you'd be willing to trade diamonds for a bottle of water. At that point, the marginal value of water is greater than the marginal value of diamonds.

What's a Professional Athlete Worth?

The value of labor works the same way. Teachers, for example, provide a tremendous amount of *total* value to society. They're passing on large amounts of information so others can be more productive. Professional athletes, however, only provide entertainment. Without professional sports, life would carry on just fine.

However, the marginal value of athletes is extremely high. I'm a huge Indianapolis Colts fan, so let's use Peyton Manning as an example. If Peyton were to come out of retirement and take snaps under center for a couple of hours against the New England Patriots, it would produce millions of dollars in ticket sales and advertising revenues. During that same time, a teacher may be able to cover the syllabus of an upcoming economics course.

The next use of a professional athlete, the marginal value, is much higher than for teachers. That's why professional athletes are paid seemingly outrageous amounts of money for "what they do."

People who believe professional athletes are paid too much, however, are basing that decision on the total values of different professions, rather than the marginal values that drive decisions.

Nobody in business is going to pay anyone any amount of money for something that creates losses. It's impossible to say that professional athletes "make too much money" since it's the market dictating the price. The reason professional athletes make so much money is that it's a reflection of the market's demand for sports. The market is just doing its job by supplying the amount of entertainment people desire.

If you think Peyton Manning makes too much money, don't look to the government to distribute some of his overage to you to make things fair. Instead, convince everyone to stop going to, watching, talking, or tweeting about NFL games or playing fantasy football. Football salaries will drop in response.

Supply and Demand Drive the Market

How do all buyers and sellers coordinate so that everyone who wants to buy something is exactly matched with someone who wishes to sell? That's Adam Smith's invisible hand at work, and it's all based on supply and demand.

Unlike the Chinese and other communist nations, under capitalism, we don't need a centralized planning committee to organize society. Instead, people just need to know one thing: price. Because we're free to set prices—and free to respond—prices send signals through the economy of what's needed most. If people start demanding more of a product or service, let's say, more beer, the price will rise as stores begin to sell out and have shortages. When stores raise their prices, they act like economists without even knowing it, and by reducing the number of buyers, they equalize the market.

But the higher price also sends a signal through the economy that more beer is needed. The market responds and delivers by creating more stores offering cases of beer. Profits provide the incentive, and we end up living in a world with Budweiser, Miller Lite, Coors, and tens of thousands of local breweries.

For example, let's take the gasoline market and assume it's in equilibrium, which means there's no buying or selling pressure. The price is holding steady at $3 per gallon, day after day. However, if OPEC decides to pump more oil and increase the supply, there's only one way to get rid of it: a lower price. Using the earlier supply and demand graphs, we can see that when supply rises, price falls. With more supply but no additional demand, you must entice people to buy the additional oil. Prices fall.

With lower prices, people find uses for that oil because the marginal value is lower. At $3 per gallon, you may use 30 gallons per week to operate your car. But if the price falls to $2, you may decide to buy another 20 gallons per week (for a total of 50 gallons) to operate something with a lower marginal value, say a boat. Alternatively, some may simply buy more fuel for their car but then use it for things they normally wouldn't, such as taking a drive up the coast on a Sunday afternoon. They chose to do these activities because they have lower marginal values compared to getting to work. Because gas is relatively cheap, they decided to do them. Price provides the incentive.

If the supply remains at these new levels, price will hold steady at $2, and the market is in a new equilibrium. But now that gas is relatively cheap, people may respond to the lower prices and create additional uses. Maybe new gasoline-powered gadgets are developed, or maybe Detroit cranks out bigger, faster, more luxurious cars with lower fuel efficiency. These new uses give people the incentive to buy *additional* gas that was never demanded before. We have a shift in demand. The demand has increased, which means the demand curve shifts upward to the right and settles at a new, higher price.

You may have demanded 30 gallons per week at $3 and a total of 50 gallons at $2. But with all the new gas-driven gadgets, you now need 75 gallons per week. Everyone else needs more too. However, if OPEC hasn't changed the supply to meet the new demands, we have an increase in price. But just like the farmer who loses a bag of grain during the night, if the price of gas rises back to $3, you don't stop buying the usual 30 gallons for your car. Instead, you quit running your new gas-driven gadgets or taking Sunday drives.

In fact, if gas prices rise even higher to $4, you may still buy 30 gallons per week to ensure you can get to work. But you may need extra money to pay for it. Where does it come from? You'll have to give up other things that have lower marginal values to you. Maybe you'll quit going to the movies, going shopping, dining out, or doing other activities that have lower marginal values to pay for the highly valued use of getting to work.

In 2008, the United States experienced some of the highest gas prices ever, with some cities nearing $5 per gallon. Many financial articles tried to make the argument that something was wrong with economic theory since there didn't appear to be fewer cars on the road despite high gas prices. With higher prices, shouldn't people do less driving?

Nothing was wrong with the theory. It was just that most people didn't understand marginal values. While gas prices were high, they weren't high enough to make people give up driving. Instead, the high prices caused people to give up nearly everything else to maintain the highly valued use of driving cars. The sharp drop in spending contributed to the Great Recession around 2008.

You can be sure, however, if gas prices continued to rise, we'd have eventually reached a point where people would begin carpooling, using public transportation, and finding other ways to get to work. That's when you'd see a reduction in traffic.

So even though $5 was historically high per gallon, it wasn't high enough to make people stop driving. Just as the farmer didn't face starvation because one bag of grain was missing, people weren't under threat of not being able to get to work just because gas was reaching $5 per gallon. Instead, people stopped doing things with lower marginal values. Figuratively, they stopped feeding pigeons.

Beer may be an oversimplified way to look at the balance and relationship in prices, but it's a basic lesson you shouldn't forget, no matter who you are or what industry you're in. People and firms want to make the most money possible, and in the long run, in a free market economy, prices will reflect the point where people and firms make the most amount of money.

It Takes Two to Tango: Part II

In chapter 2, we talked about the interaction between buyers and sellers that drives the economy. Supply and demand graphs show the details of those interactions. However, the market price is never just about supply or just about demand in isolation. It's the *interaction* between supply and demand that determines price.

If you're like my boys and me and have ever watched the TV show Pawn Stars or programs like it, you know that just because something is rare doesn't make it valuable. Something that's in extremely short supply will have no value if there's no demand.

As a Millennial, I got to live through the hardware evolution of computers. We went from 5 ¼-inch to 3 1/2-inch computer floppy disks to Zip disks before USB flash drives flooded the market. Floppy disks are nearly impossible to find these days, but if you do find one, chances are you won't even be able to give it away. Nobody wants it. Not long ago I found some disks in a box with some of my old college textbooks, and my oldest son didn't even know what it was.

All too often, people believe that if something is in short supply, it must have a high price, but that's simply not true. It will have a high price only if there's also a large group of people willing to pay dearly for it.

Conversely, just because something has a relatively large supply doesn't necessarily mean it carries a cheap price tag. Diamonds are in far higher supply than 3 ½-inch floppy disks. However, diamonds command much higher premiums because there's a bigger demand. People are willing to pay more.

What about demand by itself? There's a very high demand for computers, but they're also pretty cheap because of all the suppliers. A high demand doesn't necessarily mean a high price.

And, finally, low demand can also create high prices. For example, if you're a car nut like me and have an older car that needs parts, you may find they carry a high price because there are so few manufacturers or no manufacturers at all. With low demand, there's no incentive to produce, so you'll end up with a high price.

In the words of economist Alfred Marshall, supply and demand are like two blades on a pair of scissors. Neither blade can cut paper by itself. It takes both. Anytime you're trying to think through economic problems, be sure to consider supply and demand together. It always takes two to tango, and, well, sex without two isn't sex. It's the interaction between supply and demand that determines price. It's the relative levels that determine whether something is in high or low demand and whether it'll carry a high or low price.

In later chapters, you'll see that if you only consider supply or demand—rather than supply and demand—you're bound to make bad economic predictions. Always remember that we live in a world of unlimited wants but with limited resources. The value of anything depends on the supply and demand—not artificial values governments may assign.

As supply and demand change, people's perceptions of value change. It's best to allow people to freely assign values to goods and services and let supply and demand dictate the price based on those values. The nation always ends up with more efficient allocations of scarce resources by letting supply and demand do the work.

CHAPTER 5

ECONOMICS OF EMPLOYMENT

Capitalism has certainly created a high standard of living for Americans. We're among the wealthiest nations on the planet and produce more goods and services than many others. But behind all the production and prosperity, there's an increasing amount of talk that the system is inherently unfair. To many, it seems that some people make way too much money while others can barely make ends meet.

In 2015, the average CEO earned over $10 million per year—more than enough to last most people a lifetime. We see professional athletes making hundreds of millions each year, living in 50,000-square-foot oceanfront mansions and traveling by private yachts and jets—all for chasing a ball. Schoolteachers, however, with years of expensive education, training, and invaluable experiences to share with tomorrow's leaders, struggle to earn $50,000 per year, the same amount some athletes earn per hour. For those at the bottom, the 2014 minimum wage rates never exceeded $10 per hour in any state. At that level, the wage rates were just enough to keep workers a step above the poverty level.

How can a system that provides such abundance for the entire nation also seem so unfair for the masses? It's for reasons like these that people are convinced something is wrong with capitalism and that the government needs to step in to make things fair. It's easy to believe the system is rigged so that big businesses get bigger and the rich get richer at everybody else's expense. But remember, it's easy to overlook the things you can't see.

The difficult story to tell is that nothing's wrong with the system, and everyone is better off compared to any other economic system. The further a nation departs from capitalism, the lower the quality of life for its citizens. Once you understand the economics of employment, you'll see why capitalism makes the most efficient use of labor and can produce more goods and services for everyone. This chapter sheds light on the pieces that are easy to overlook.

Productivity Is Key

Prosperity depends on one thing: productivity. The more goods and services produced, the more there is available to go around to everyone. As productivity increases, the Law of Supply states that price will fall and more people can afford to have those goods or services.

Most people, however, believe that jobs are the key. They focus on money and think prosperity depends on spending. It's easy to think this because you can see it. You can buy lots of things if you have money. In a nation with an abundance of goods and services, you're not alone in thinking that money is the driving force that makes the world go around. However, money is only a way to facilitate trade and make it easier to exchange goods without resorting to barter, swapping apples for bananas, for instance.

I had a consultant who worked for me back when I owned a wholesale distribution company. He traveled the world as we set up our supply chain, and he said the oddest thing he found about traveling the globe, from the hottest desert to the coldest regions in Russia, is that you can always find ripe, yellow bananas wherever you go. Why is this?

All the money in the world can't buy a thing if nothing's produced. If everyone in the nation earned millions of dollars each year, nobody would be better off if there was nothing to buy. Money doesn't create prosperity, but as long as there is demand for bananas, you will always be able to buy them in all corners of the world.

People see money as the key to prosperity because we already have lots of things produced. The fact is, however, it's just the opposite: the reason we have prosperity is that we've efficiently produced lots of goods and services to go around. The only reason people want money is to buy goods and services, whether today or by saving for the future. Any motive for earning money is ultimately tied to buying things.

Do More Jobs Lead to More Prosperity?

Any economic policies that focus on the number of jobs or the wages paid is missing the point of prosperity. Jobs only matter if people are working efficiently to produce things everybody wants. Jobs are not the issue as they arise all by themselves from economic necessity.

There is technically never any shortage of jobs. We can create all the jobs we want—as long as we're willing to do things inefficiently. For instance, we could create lots of jobs by enacting laws that ban the use of computers, machinery, factories, and other tools that allow us to produce things quickly and cheaply. We'd instantly need many more people to get things done, but the economy would never be able to produce the same amount of output after the bans.

Imagine, rather than harvesting millions of acres of corn using massive John Deere diesel combines, a law could require farms to hire thousands of people at high wages to pick corn kernel by kernel with a pair of tweezers. We'd see millions of people working, and all those workers would end up with lots of money in their pockets. We would believe we were heading for better times—until we arrived at the market and found we had very little corn to sell.

The price of corn would then skyrocket, which in turn would cause other prices to rise. The price of beef would rise, since farmers would have to pay more for corn to feed cattle. Because it would then cost more to raise cattle, fewer cattle would be raised, thus causing the cost of leather to skyrocket, and on and on until most people would be left without. Despite all the jobs and money gained by putting people to work harvesting corn, we'd be worse off.

We could ban the use of cell phones and emails and require you to hire someone to write your message, another to encrypt it, another to carry it by horseback to the recipient, and another to decode the message and read it. It's a strategy that would employ many people, but does it sound like we'd make tremendous economic progress?

Do you think all those new jobs would create more goods and services? Or do you think we'd end up with a severe shortage of other things and be worse off? I'll say it again: there is no shortage of jobs.

There is, however, a shortage of resources, which is exactly the problem that we economists try to solve. It's not jobs we should be after; it's opportunity. We don't gain anything by simply creating jobs. Instead, if we want prosperity and higher standards of living, we must create productive jobs that also make the best use of scarce resources. We need machines and techniques that produce more goods and services to go around for everyone. It doesn't come from a bunch of people idly standing around with paper money in their pockets but nothing to buy.

An efficient nation that produces more will always have a higher standard of living for all its citizens. Productivity leads to more goods and services, lower prices, and higher standards of living. Everyone benefits.

Once you realize jobs aren't the issue, it shouldn't matter who produces the goods and services as long as they can produce a lot to go around for everyone. Focus on productivity, and prosperity follows. This is why economists are in favor of countries that can produce things the cheapest.

If Mexico could produce all the cars the United States needs for one dollar each, why should we block those imports on the grounds that it's unfair to American auto workers? Import the cars and cross them off the list of things we need to produce. Everybody could easily own a brand-new car and have lots of money left over. Perhaps we could then shift the unused resources—factories, labor, and materials—to making boats. Everyone could have a new car *plus* a new boat. We'd be better off.

As we talked about in chapter 1, as long as trade is free and fair, then anytime someone (or another country) is willing to offer the same goods or services for less money, we should take it.

Mexican imports don't create permanent unemployment here. They only cause people to shift to producing other needed goods and services. But because additional boats, or other goods, never get produced, we overlook them and say the cheap auto imports were harmful to the American economy. It's true that auto workers will have fewer dollars in their pockets in the short run as they turn their skills to producing different goods. However, with any policy, we must always ask if the benefits are greater than the costs.

Economists assume that everyone matters equally, so although auto workers may end up with lower incomes, the vast majority of US citizens gain benefits. If the benefits are greater than the costs, it's a policy that should be adopted. It doesn't make sense for 1% of the population to benefit at the expense of the remaining 99%.

A new rising industry is that of 3-D printing. A few firms are printing airplane parts that are stronger, lighter, and far cheaper. Research is showing that we may be able to print commercial jets for a fraction of the cost of traditional methods. Will we be worse off if we can conduct face-to-face business around the world at a fraction of the cost? Or would we be better off lobbying policy to prevent the expansion of the industry and cause the entire world to face higher prices so that a few airlines can make more money? Even if 3-D printing destroys current airline firms as we know them, it will inevitably create new industries for many to be employed. In the end, the majority of people are far better off. What if you could print your dream home for pennies? Should we ban the technology?

A similar thing is happening with Uber, the online taxi company that allows anyone to register to use their car to drive others on demand. By using a free phone app, anyone can "call" a taxi to nearly any location and get quick, reliable transportation at a fraction of the cost traditional taxis charge. Hundreds of unemployed people are now able to become self-employed drivers, and the rest of the world benefits from lower prices.

Naturally, there's uproar from the current guard, the traditional taxi companies that enjoyed higher prices before Uber, but we should never consider progress—more goods and services at lower prices—as a form of destruction. Productivity is the key, and we should never block an industry, or country, that can provide better goods and services—or cheaper ones.

Would we be better off today if we had blocked the invention of the automobile on the grounds that it would hurt the horse and buggy industry? Or the invention of cell phones because they would hurt the phone booth industry? Or ban email because it harms the postal service? Yet that's exactly the argument people are making when they say we're worse off because of Chinese imports.

At a household level, it would be hard to convince families they should pay $100 per hour for an adult babysitter when teenagers are willing to do it for far less. You couldn't persuade people to hire the adult and pay higher prices just because it would provide an adult with a job. But change the wording to say we should "hire" US auto workers to produce cars, even though we can get them far cheaper from Mexico, and everyone votes for the policy. It's easy to believe damage is done because most people focus on the lost jobs and incomes of auto workers. They only account for costs. You must think past that and understand there are far more benefits to most citizens if we import cars from Mexico. We're always better off with cheaper things—cars included. We must let the unused talent shift to producing things we don't have.

When I started working on my first trading floor out of college, our phones rang 24 hours a day. Prior to the Internet, individual retail investors had to trade stock through stockbrokers, who collected hundreds of dollars in commissions. Now the same stock trades can be made for just a few dollars. Yes, many stockbrokers and trading houses went bust, but that's productivity. Many more people are now able to invest because investing is cheaper. That's prosperity.

Raise the Minimum Wage

If you listen to the popular press and politicians regarding minimum wage, you'll get a message that runs opposite of good economic theory. Politicians don't think about productivity. Rather, they think about jobs and money. They'll convince you that money is what's important and we need to increase the number of jobs—and the minimum wage.

We're hearing it now with millions of people screaming that minimum wages are too low, and Washington is responding. In the 2014 State of the Union address, President Obama asked for national minimum wage rates to be lifted from $7.25 to $10.10 an hour. The Seattle City Council took a bigger step and voted to hike rates to $15 per hour over the next several years. In a July 2015 *Time* article, Hillary Clinton outlined her economic vision with a focus on income and how paychecks must grow for the middle class. Her economic plan centered on job creation.

In a 2015 CNN.com article, Mary Kay Henry, president of the Service Employees International Union (SEIU), expressed her opinions that home healthcare wages must be increased to $15 per hour to allow workers to raise their families with dignity. She also added that everyone benefits since these workers have more money to spend, which gets filtered back to big businesses. (Ironically, she contradicts herself in other articles about her relentless fight for affordable healthcare because something must be done about the spiraling out-of-control costs.)

My fellow Indiana businessman David Bego wrote a book, *The Devil at Our Doorstep*, about his company, EMS, and their fight with the SEIU as SEIU worked to unionize his cleaning company, even though his company paid above-market wages. As Bego found out, facts are not something that those who fight for a higher minimum wage use in their claims.

There are no shortages of bad economics at work in the minimum wage debate, and they all carry the same tune: raising the minimum wage for low-paying jobs benefits everyone because workers will have more money in their pockets, and big businesses will prosper from the increased spending. It's an easy story to sell to the public. It seems so logical and obvious to those in favor of increased minimum wages that they can't understand what's wrong with those who are strongly opposed.

Those in favor of the increased wages think big businesses are just tight with the money. Disgruntled workers might say to themselves, "These businesses want more money for themselves and their overpriced CEOs. They can afford to pay more to workers, but just choose not to because they're too big and powerful and can influence laws to keep wages low."

The solution seems obvious: the government needs to step in and make things fair. By forcing a higher minimum wage for low-skilled workers, the playing field is leveled and everyone will be better off. It sounds like a good idea, but raising the minimum wage will have severe unintended consequences. Remember how you can create a plague of deadly cobras when the government tweaks prices and changes incentives? It's the same story with wages.

We can call it a minimum wage, but it's a price nonetheless—the minimum price of labor. As we found in chapter 4, the Law of Demand states that as prices rise, people buy fewer goods and services. So, as the price of labor rises, businesses will naturally respond by hiring fewer workers. Which workers get laid off? The ones most skilled and productive or those with a smaller range of skills? It will naturally be those with low skills, exactly those the minimum wage laws were intended to help.

In a 2016 interview, Emil Brolick, CEO of Wendy's hamburger chain, stated that higher minimum wages would mean focusing on installing more self-order kiosks and automating more restaurant kitchens. That day has already come for some businesses. The Walmart my grandmother worked in has switched to— yep, you guessed it—self-checkout lines. The newly rebuilt McDonald's in my hometown includes—yep, you guessed it—self-ordering kiosks. In other words, businesses respond to higher-priced labor by hiring fewer people.

As for Wendy's, it's already looking at reducing overall staff and hours, in addition to raising prices. "Unfortunately, we believe that some of these increases will clearly end up hurting the people they're intended to help," says Brolick.

The minimum wage can be increased to $15 per hour, but don't be fooled into thinking everyone who wants to work for that amount will get hired. The government can't require businesses to employ everyone who wants a job. Instead, the government can require a business to pay more money if it chooses to hire a worker. That's entirely different. The day the law gets passed isn't the day all minimum-wage employees get more money. It's the day most will get laid off.

People are already responding before the law is even in effect. On July 23, 2015, New York's state wage board recommended that fast-food workers make at least $15 per hour by 2018. In a press conference, Dunkin' Donuts CEO Nigel

Travis said the plan will do more harm than good and probably force Dunkin' to lay off workers—exactly what we economists predict.

Proponents for a higher minimum wage think the government will force businesses to pay all existing workers more money because it's fair. Not true. The laws just change the incentives, and businesses will respond by hiring fewer people.

But it gets worse. With a higher price, the Law of Supply says that more people will be willing to supply labor. In other words, with a higher minimum wage, more new job seekers appear. They'll be ones who feel their labor is worth $15 per hour, which means they're more skilled than those currently working in those positions.

The higher minimum wage is simply going to increase the talent level and weed out the very people it was intended to help. With more people willing to work, coupled with businesses willing to hire fewer people, the unemployment rate will rise.

Will Higher Wages Improve the Economy?

Okay, so maybe not everyone will have a job, but those who do will have more money. Higher minimum wage supporters believe everyone will benefit since it increases the amount of spending in the economy. The idea is that people will spend more, and as businesses enjoy increased sales, they will have more money to expand operations. More people will be hired. A virtuous cycle of prosperity results, right?

But will businesses sell more and create more prosperity? If a business paid a worker $10 per hour but now must pay her $15 per hour, where does the money come from? It comes from the business. If the wage increase puts another $1,000 in the employee's pocket each month, it's exactly $1,000 taken from the business. The employee may be able to spend an extra $1,000, but the *business* is prevented from spending $1,000.

The increased minimum wage laws will change who gets to spend the money, but it doesn't change the amount of money or the amount of spending in the system. It's not possible to make everyone better off by simply shifting money around. You can't make yourself wealthier by transferring money from your savings to your checking account each month. You can't increase the amount of money your household can spend by increasing your children's allowance.

Yet that's the essence of the argument by those who believe prosperity will result if businesses are forced to pay higher minimum wages. If prosperity could be created by simply raising the minimum wage, why stop at $15 per hour? Why not $20, $100, or $1,000 per hour? If everyone benefits from higher wages, then let's make it a number with serious punch.

The fact that those who argue in favor of higher wages also put a cap on it, say $15, is a sign they can't possibly believe their own words. Instead, what they're really suggesting is their opinion of a "fair" price is better than what was reached by the collective actions of people: the market price.

Once the minimum wage is increased, tens of thousands of people will be instantly unemployed, losing their homes, cars, and other assets. If one of those unemployed would be thrilled to have a job for $14 per hour to save her from bankruptcy, the government says you're not allowed to employ them. By creating a $15 minimum wage, the government is saying that no business is allowed to hire anyone not worth at least $15 per hour.

The nation loses productivity—prosperity—by having all those people unemployed. The higher minimum wage will create higher unemployment and fewer goods and services in the process.

Look what happened among professional positions where employees screamed for mandatory health benefits. The government responded and now makes health benefits a requirement that businesses must provide if they have more than 50 full-time employees.

How did businesses respond? They didn't hire as many employees. Instead, they hired independent 1099 contractors who aren't technically employees. These "contractors" still go to work each day, as they always did, park in the same spaces, sit at the same desks, and have the same responsibilities. The difference is that the laws have now caused businesses to label them as "contractors," not "employees."

In most corporations, if an employee works more than 40 hours per week, it makes her a full-time worker and eligible for benefits. With the rise of contract work, overtime pay is disappearing into history. With the new laws, not only do the employees not have the health benefits they demanded, but they also don't have the security of full-time employment or the ability to work overtime. They're worse off.

Increasing the minimum wage only gives a different set of incentives: businesses will hire fewer employees, yet more people will enter the workforce. We'll have more unemployed people.

The Costs of Higher Minimum Wages

Will anyone benefit from higher minimum wages? There's no question that the relatively few employed people will be better off. But whenever you analyze any policy, you can't just focus on the benefits. You must also consider the costs. If the costs are greater than the benefits, it's not a good policy.

With higher minimum wages, not only will many low-skilled workers lose their jobs, but the entire nation must now pay higher prices. For example, if McDonald's is forced to pay higher wages, it will charge more for hamburgers and fries. So every McDonald's patron now has fewer dollars to spend elsewhere. Again, a higher minimum wage doesn't put more money into the economic system and create an ever-increasing spiral of prosperity. All it does is shift the spending to other people.

With higher prices, McDonald's will also face reduced sales. This, of course, is where those in favor of minimum wage hikes feel it's a better policy. They think McDonald's and all its high-paid upper management will easily get by with reduced sales. The CEO will live just fine on $9 million per year while all those low-skilled workers can finally enjoy a higher standard of living. But reducing one person's salary by a few million per year isn't going to put a dent in the additional labor costs that rise by 50% or more for every franchise in the nation.

The money must come from somewhere, so McDonald's will search for other areas to cut costs. Perhaps the company will choose to cut or eliminate its dividend to shareholders. Doing so reduces the amount of income to many retirees, pension funds, and those who hold the company's shares. With a smaller dividend, McDonald's stock price will likely fall, thus harming the 401(k) plans of every McDonald's employee in the world.

Higher minimum wages may therefore make a few employees better off today, but the majority will be worse off in the long run. McDonald's may also cut its hours of operations, which will also reduce its revenues and further lower its stock price. With lower revenues and shorter hours of operations, fewer employees get hired. These possibilities, however, are overlooked since people in favor of higher minimum wages think it's simply a way of forcing companies to pay more money. They assume nothing else changes.

Prices send signals through the economy—and people respond. McDonald's must get the money from somewhere, so it will likely raise prices and cut costs, which sends a ripple through the entire economy. Everything is connected to everything else, and it's easy to forget about all the moving parts, especially those you can't see. But make no mistake about it, raising the minimum wage will create greater costs than benefits.

The fast food argument is often used, as the industry employs so many minimum wage workers, but many people won't notice or change consumption if the price of a burger and fries increased by 29 cents. What about service-based businesses with the majority of their costs based on labor expenses? The effects of an increased minimum wage will have a big impact on industries where workers earn wages higher than the current minimum but below the new minimum wage.

For example, let's look at the daycare business that my wife and I used to own. In the childcare industry, the average national tuition for center-based daycare is just under $1,000 per month per child, with the cost of labor making up about 60% of the expenses for childcare. If the average cost of a daycare teacher is currently $10 per hour and would increase to $15 per hour, then to maintain the same amount of margin above labor expenses, the childcare center would have to increase tuition to $1,300 per month.

Many families couldn't afford an increase of $300 per month for childcare. Mothers who previously worked and sent their kids to daycare may have to quit their jobs to stay home with the children. Fewer kids would be in daycare, and preschool teachers would lose their jobs.

What about the other effects of not having an affordable childcare system? The long-term, trickle-down effects on the economy would have a much greater impact than daycare workers losing their job. What about the loss to society as children no longer get the same head start to education they previously had? What if, due to the high cost of childcare, families decide to only have one child instead of two?

As an economist, you must look past the simple costs of a program or policy and understand that more is at stake. As you can see, a change in the minimum wage could end up lowering the birth rate and education level of an entire generation of Americans.

Prices and Signals

Economists have warned about problems with creating artificially high minimum wages. While higher wages do provide more income for a select few, they also create a signal for the rest of the economy.

The nation needs a certain number of doctors, lawyers, managers, artists, singers, musicians, and any number of possible careers. We don't need everyone to be a teacher or everyone to be a basketball player. But it's not possible to assume that people will naturally gravitate to the careers the nation needs.

So how do we make sure we have just the right amount of people in each profession? We do that with price. The only way for people to voluntarily channel themselves into the correct number of industries is to let prices dictate what's needed.

If there's a shortage of doctors, salaries will rise, and people will respond by entering the profession. If there's a shortage of accountants, salaries rise, and more people enter the field. On the flipside, if there are too many pilots, salaries fall, and people leave or choose not to enter. Prices allow the nation to send signals to everyone about what jobs are needed and where.

You can't have a system where all jobs pay well because then there's no incentive, yet that's what politicians are trying to do by raising the minimum wage. With higher minimum wages, people will shift to those jobs since they're now relatively more attractive.

An entry-level manager earning a fixed salary equal to $15 per hour may find it's not worth the long hours and hard work when he could become a busboy for the same pay. Commercial window washers earning $20 per hour may find it's more attractive to be a busboy for $15 per hour and not have to suspend themselves from a rope on a 50-story building. It may seem better to earn a little less money but keep both feet on the ground.

All prices are relative. When one price is changed, all other prices rise or fall in relative terms. For example, if busboys earn $5 per hour and managers earn $20 per hour, busboys earn 25% of what managers earn, and managers earn four times more than busboys. There's a big—and appropriate—incentive for busboys to gain skills and become managers.

But if the minimum wage rises to $15 for busboys, they now earn 75% of what managers earn, while managers only earn 1.3 times that of busboys. In relative terms, it's far more attractive to remain or become a busboy. There's no longer much of an incentive to work hard to become a manager, even though that's what's needed. At the same time, there's an incentive for some managers to take a little less pay but have less demanding work and more free time.

Will managers' salaries be proportionally increased? No, because the laws only apply to those making minimum wage. So the minimum-wage jobs become relatively more attractive if all other wages or salaries stay the same. More people will shift to them, even though the economy would benefit from people shifting *out* of minimum-wage roles into more productive roles. Therefore, the overall economy will become less productive with the proposed increase in minimum wage.

If we have wages and salaries to compare, the market will naturally balance the right number of people in the right number of positions. Raising the minimum wage only forces more people into jobs the nation doesn't need. It's counterproductive, regardless of all the people who like to make a big deal about the jobs that would be created.

Always remember that prices send signals, and to gain prosperity, we need to send the right signals to the right markets. Remember, we need opportunities, not jobs.

Minimum-Wage Jobs Are Not Careers

Minimum-wage jobs were never intended to be careers. They're simple positions that help young kids contribute to productivity and gain experience.

In the process, the entire nation benefits by having more—and cheaper—goods and services to go around. That's productivity that results in a higher standard of living for everyone.

This is why the argument about the *need* for higher minimum wages so that people can raise families with dignity has no economic merit. It's not that we wouldn't like to see everyone have high-paying jobs, but it's just not possible to pay everyone equal amounts, regardless of the work produced.

To ask everyone in the nation to pay far more for goods and services so we can create careers out of any position is asking everyone to engage in charity. There's nothing wrong with charity, but you shouldn't expect people to respond by asking them to tip hundred-dollar bills for a cup of coffee so that everyone can be better off. Yet that's what's happening when politicians support high minimum wages. They're asking the entire nation to be worse off so that less than 1% of the population can enjoy a higher standard of living.

Instead, the economy must set labor prices according to needs. If there's an increased need for teachers, salaries will naturally rise and send a signal through the economy that we need more educators. People will respond.

But if we fiddle with prices and increase the pay for low-skilled jobs, it creates the wrong incentives. Politicians and mainstream media overlook that. They make it sound as if everyone doing some kind of work—no matter what— must be able to afford a house, family, cars, vacations, children's education, and retirement savings.

People are always better off making their own deals. If McDonald's is willing to make an offer for entry-level employment at $7 per hour and people respond by filling out applications, why is it wrong? Is it right for the government to say it's not fair for two parties to make an agreement where both feel they're better off? If, on the other hand, McDonald's can't hire enough people at $7 per hour, it has no choice but to offer higher wages. The number will naturally rise by itself if there's a need.

Let's describe this a different way and see how you'd respond. What if the government said that the very cheapest restaurant food must cost a minimum of $30 per meal to ensure that all restaurants have some basic level of revenue to make things fair. Would you take a date to McDonald's and spend $60 for a couple of Happy Meals? Or, for the same money, would you go to a finer restaurant? The law wouldn't help McDonald's in the least. In fact, it would do the most harm by causing people to no longer eat there. Any such law would do nothing but drive people to higher-quality establishments. If you're forced to spend at least $30 per meal, you may as well get your money's worth.

Expect businesses to respond to increased labor costs exactly the same way you would to mandatory minimum food prices. Businesses will shift to higher-skilled workers.

You can be sure McDonald's would lobby hard against any such legislation that would raise prices to $30 per meal. But change the wording of that legislation of $30 meals to "increasing minimum wages" and low-skilled workers wouldn't be able to get in line fast enough to vote yes. If they understood economics, they'd vote to turn it down. It doesn't make sense to vote yourself out of a job.

Who's the Judge?

Low-skilled workers want the government to step in to make things fair, but who should be the judge as to what's fair? What makes people think the government knows everybody's needs and can unequivocally say that $15 is fair for all minimum levels of work? If you're perfectly willing to work for $14 per hour and someone offers it to you, why is that unfair? If you don't like the offer, you can always say no. However, with higher minimum wages, you're not allowed to say yes to a lower wage.

And if we're going to have the government tell us what a fair minimum is, why don't we look to the government to have fair maximums? Why don't people say that it's unfair for Louis Vuitton to charge $1,000 for a handbag? Or for Jimmy Buffett to charge my fellow Parrotheads hundreds for a concert ticket? In reality, people are better off deciding for themselves, without the government's help. If Jimmy can't sell all seats at the asking price, the promoters will lower prices. If there are still people standing in line—ahem, still searching for seats on the Internet—when the last ticket is sold, expect prices to rise.

When the price is right, everyone who wants a ticket for that price will get one. There will be no shortages or surpluses, and the market is balanced. Who do you think is in a better position to determine the right price for Jimmy Buffett concerts: the promoters or the government? The ticket's value depends on the month, day, time, and of course seat. It would be a disaster for the government to try to set a single fair price for every ticket.

The promoters, however, will probably get the price nearly perfect every single time. Concert promoters are far more in touch with supply and demand for various times and venues; they understand, better than the government, all factors necessary to determine the clearing price. The market will take care of itself and establish the fairest price between buyers and sellers.

There's a clever saying in the law business: a good lawyer knows the law, but an excellent lawyer knows the judge. Make sure you're confident in the person you're appointing as judge of your values. An economist would say you're the best person to make that decision, which is why countries thrive under capitalism. But if you listen to most people today, they're all voting for the government to sit on the bench and decide which prices *you* are allowed to bargain with.

It doesn't take a jury to figure out that's a terribly inefficient system. However, there are some cases, such as in a monopoly, where government involvement may actually be beneficial.

Who Should Determine Minimum Wages?

As one of the wealthiest nations, we should strive for higher standards of living. Nobody would argue that we'd like to see everyone living the best life possible. Remember, though, economics is concerned with making the best use of scarce resources. We can't have it all. It's unrealistic to think we can create higher standards of living for everyone just by altering the minimum price of labor. So what's the next best thing?

Understand that capitalists create jobs. It's easy to look at a Microsoft, McDonald's, or Walmart and think the reason they exist is to provide jobs for everyone. They are instead businesses created by individuals. The owners have every right to decide how much they're willing to pay for labor, just as you can decide how much you're willing to pay for babysitters or lawn care.

The nation's wealth is largely due to capitalists who use scarce resources efficiently. Henry Ford's automobile, Alexander Graham Bell's telephone, Thomas Edison's light bulb, and Sam Walton's stores were all the result of people in pursuit of profits. These individuals created better lives for themselves for one reason only: they made things everybody wanted.

Bill Gates's vast wealth is a direct result of the benefits he created for the world. While he's worth nearly $90 billion, it pales in comparison to the wealth he's created for others. Just think of all the jobs worldwide that were created because of his innovation—everything from programming and consulting to instruction, software, computer repair, and so much more. If you take away the incentive for people to create and invent, you shrink the size of the pie (national production).

In other words, it may seem like people are better off if they earn more money per hour, but you're overlooking the power of incentives when the market is at work without government interference. You'll get far fewer capitalists when restrictions and laws are placed on wage and profit. Minimum-wage employees may feel like they're getting more slices of pie, but the slices will be far smaller. Overall, it's a net loss.

The problem isn't that these companies pay their workers too little; the problem is that we have too many people willing to do the work. If we create artificially high wages, we don't use all of the nation's labor efficiently to produce more goods and services. Capitalists can't create businesses as efficiently with higher costs. In the long run, the nation's productivity slows.

It's an illusion that we're creating wealth by increasing minimum wages. Even Walmart is jumping on the bandwagon with a new campaign about how it cares for its employees by increasing minimum wages. The campaign features the tagline, "We all benefit from higher minimum wages."

My grandma worked at Walmart for 18 years after she retired. She loved meeting and talking to people in the community. People would wait extra just to go through her checkout line so they could talk to her. She loved her job, and Walmart was very good to her. However, the reason Walmart is raising minimum wages is not from the goodness of its corporate heart. It's being forced, so it may as well make the best of a bad situation and make it look like it's helping the community. It's an advertising ploy to get people to shop there in support of its "new standards."

But be sure the company will respond by hiring fewer people. And those hired will be highly skilled so executives can justify the price they pay for wages. Walmart has shifted, and will continue to shift, to self-checkout lines, and the conversations you used to have with my grandma and other Walmart employees about the weather or the graduation party you're buying supplies for will become a thing of the past.

The reality is that only a small percentage of people will benefit from the minimum-wage laws. The rest of the nation suffers by having fewer jobs—and paying higher prices. We all overlook the things we can't see.

Imagine how the country would look today if we didn't have the automobile, airplane, electricity, television, light bulbs, computers, and all the other inventions that have created the nation's wealth. We'd still be living with *Little House on the Prairie* technology. But because we've become accustomed to such high standards of living, we overlook what could have been and say the capitalists are making things unfair.

We must keep things in perspective and realize that 70% of the world lives on $10 per day—not $15 per hour. We still have one of the highest standards of living, which is why so many people still want to come to the United States to pursue their American dream.

If the government shouldn't determine minimum wages, then who should? Wages, like any price, are best determined by supply and demand. They're determined by those who are willing to buy and sell labor at a given price. If wages are free to fluctuate, then people who are willing to perform the work for less money, say $10 per hour, will show up to fill out applications. They'll be happy, and the nation will benefit from cheaper prices.

Being able to offer services for less money gives the worker bargaining power to compete for the job. But if the government takes that away, it removes the only weapon the worker had to fight for the job. By forcing a higher minimum wage, $15 for example, the government is effectively saying that anyone who wishes to work for less than $15 is not allowed to.

My grandmother never made $15 per hour, even after 18 years at Walmart, and it didn't matter to her. It seems that the government is acting in the best interest of minimum-wage employees, but it's only helping those who are worth at least $15 per hour. All others will be priced out of the market.

For the proponents of higher minimum wages who boast about wanting to be fair, there's not a single thing they could do to make things more unfair.

What Determines Your Value?

Some people believe the value of any product depends on how much labor was used to create it, which is an outdated idea called the *Labor Theory of Value*. According to the theory, if you spend $3 for lemons, $2 for sugar, and $1 for a gallon of water to make lemonade, then that's $6 worth of ingredients. If your time was worth $1 to concoct the drink, then the lemonade should cost $7 per gallon. In other words, the value of anything is strictly based on the ingredients that went into it, plus some cost of labor.

It doesn't take much thought to realize this can't be right. Using this theory, if a brain surgeon spends $500 for a strip of the finest Italian leather, imports it on a private jet, and fashions it into a buggy whip, it must be worth thousands of dollars. It's as if all those costs and time magically get rolled into the perceived value of the product. Yet nobody uses buggy whips anymore. We need fuel to power our cars faster, not whips to make our horses pull buggies faster. Buggy whips have no value. The market doesn't care about the seller's costs and time. It's only concerned with the perceived value in use.

If businesses could regulate the market price strictly by how much money is spent in the creation, people would have every incentive to create things as inefficiently as possible and get into a "my costs are higher than your costs" game. We'd waste resources, produce less, and have outrageously high price tags on everything. But it should now be clear that, to advance society and make everyone better off, we need competition to see who can manufacture goods efficiently for less money.

Once you eliminate the Labor Theory of Value as a way to value goods and services, it's easy to understand why people pay thousands of dollars for an oil painting but not so much for someone to dig a ditch in the hot sun. The painting has almost no intrinsic value; it's just canvas and a little bit of paint. However, it can certainly be worth many times more than something that requires many hours of backbreaking labor. The value has nothing to do with the amount of work that goes into it. Instead, the buyer must figure out how much value there is in enjoying a beautiful piece of art compared to having dirt moved a few feet.

This is also why a higher minimum wage law isn't economically supported by saying, "These are hardworking people," or, "They deserve to raise families with dignity." The question comes down to this: how much is the good or service that results from their labor worth to the buyer?

When my grandmother passed away, literally hundreds of people in the community called, sent cards, and came to the funeral. There was even a letter to the editor in the local newspaper about how she brightened people's day when they came through her line at Walmart. But what is the value people place on having a smiling cashier over scanning their own purchases?

If the restaurant doesn't value a busboy taking dishes off a table and moving them to the kitchen at $15 per hour, you can be sure the market will respond—and eliminate the job. Why do you think people pump their own gasoline in states that don't have laws against it?

Buyers are willing to spend based on a subjective valuation. Sellers can offer goods at various prices, but nobody can force people to buy. If a buyer and seller agree, a sale is made. The value of those goods and services, however, should be up to the buyer and seller—not the government.

If the government truly wanted to help certain people with minimum skills, it's best to do it through the tax system. It's much more efficient to transfer exactly the amount of money necessary to bring about a minimum standard of living. It's terribly inefficient to raise the minimum price at which people are allowed to work, forcing far more people out of a job as a result.

What ultimately determines your value is not the job you do or how backbreaking the labor may be. Instead, it's about how easily you can be replaced. If the price of labor gets too high, it may become more economical for a business owner to make a capital investment and replace humans with new software, a machine, or a robot.

It's very easy to replace a busboy. Anybody can do the job instantly without training. If one quits, it doesn't take a manager long to find another one to replace him. It's not that the work isn't hard; it just isn't hard to find replacements. The job shouldn't command a high price. If the price of busboys gets too high, just like in states where you can pump your own gasoline, restaurants will require you to bus your own dishes, or maybe they'll buy a busboy robot that automatically collects and washes dishes.

But let's take another look at professional sports figures, who are often accused of making too much money. If you paid $100 for a goose that lays a $10,000 golden egg, it would be hard for your friends to convince you that you paid too much. Yet that's the argument people are making when they say professional athletes make too much money.

There's no doubt that if the NFL couldn't give tickets away for free, you'd see players' salaries dry up. The NFL doesn't pay players too much; instead, it pays them a salary that's just high enough to make it worth each franchise's team to stay in business. When people argue that players make too much money, what they're really saying is they want to have all their games provided for less money. The fans are saying, we want the same level of entertainment and quality, but we don't want to pay the price. They want it all for less. Don't expect the market to respond.

Similarly, each cast member of my all-time favorite show, The Simpsons, makes $300,000 per episode. Each character may only speak a few words during the 20-minute episode, which leads some to ask, how hard is that? Why should they get so much just for making funny cartoon voices? Just as with professional sports teams, the show has raked in billions of dollars for decades. Rather than saying the cast is paid too much, ask how hard it would be to replace those iconic voices. If you can't replace them, the entire franchise dries up. It's better for Fox to pay each cast member the $300k per episode and be happy with a little less revenue than have the show canceled and get zero revenue from the show.

Don't be fooled into thinking that just because you spend a lot of time and money on something—including a high-priced diploma—it automatically means you're going to earn a lot of money. It's foolish to think that if you spend hundreds of thousands on a couple of degrees that an employer must pay you more. Remember, buyers don't care about your costs; they only care about the benefits your goods or services provide.

It's always better to develop marketable skills. Most of the time, you'll need some type of degree to compete in today's market. But, more important, always ask, what does the market need now? Is it more healthcare workers? More computer programmers? Find the hot jobs and develop those specialized skills.

Don't rely on the government to make things fair by tweaking prices; don't erroneously believe the government can raise everyone's standard of living. And don't expect the government to require employers to pay economists the same wage as NFL players.

Economists against raising the minimum wage are not cold-hearted. They're just saying that it's not the solution to improving everyone's standard of living. It will backfire in a major way. In fact, not only are businesses responding by hiring fewer workers, citizens are responding too. There's now a Facebook page called "Why I Don't Tip in Seattle" where supporters leave the following card on the table rather than a tip:

Why I don't tip in Seattle

Economics 101: As the compensation for your services increases, there is a cost to me as the consumer to pay for that increase. As I have no control over the Seattle City Council's decision to redistribute wealth, I can only exercise the rights left to me.

(1) I can choose to not eat out. (Then who would pay your wages?)
(2) I can choose to be carrion for the City Council's vultures.
(3) I can choose not to tip and explain why and provide a free economics lesson.

It is not about your service. Feel free to comment/vent at "Why I don't tip in Seattle" on Facebook.

Not only is the public responding to higher minimum wages, but so are the employees, and in unexpected ways.

Nora Gibson sits on the board of the Seattle Housing Authority but is also the director for Full Life Care, a non-profit organization that provides nursing facilities. She told local television station KIRO-7 that she got unexpected reactions from workers as soon as the $11 minimum went into effect in April 2015. Some of the employees at her 24-hour care facilities asked for *reduced* hours. Huh? Turns out they wanted their hours reduced for fear the higher wages would make them ineligible for their subsidized housing.

With the higher minimums, fewer businesses will hire, but for the few employees who do get hired, it looks like they will want to work fewer hours to control their total amount of income. Thus, businesses will end up with fewer employees and fewer jobs to offer, and everyone will be worse off. Chalk up another unintended consequence from trying to manipulate the market into providing prosperity to everyone at no cost.

States that adopt increased minimum wage laws will undoubtedly see higher unemployment rates. Further, businesses that can't afford to operate at those prices will pack up and leave, thus putting even more people out of work.

Just as in all areas of economics, it's usually best to let the market decide what something is worth. Only then can we exactly balance the scarce supply of goods and services to the demand. Artificially raising or lowering prices inevitably makes things worse off. Employment is no exception.

CHAPTER 6

ECONOMICS OF GOVERNMENT SPENDING AND REGULATIONS

F ree markets efficiently provide the goods and services people need. To do that, however, entrepreneurs take risks and use their time, money, or other resources to produce those goods and services. As I've already shared, I know firsthand those risks, as not every business venture pans out.

For instance, the store owner in chapter 4 who sells beer had to use his own money or borrow money from a bank to stock cases in the first place. He also bought or leases space in the shopping plaza and accordingly gets certain rights: he may use the property to sell beer or serve food, perhaps sublease it to another tenant, hang signs on it, or paint it. He can also give it a unique name, perhaps Campus Brew. But how can he protect his rights? How can he be sure the plaza management rental company doesn't boot him out next month because they found another tenant who's willing to pay more for the space? And if his store is successful, how can he be sure another person doesn't open a store with the identical name to steal his customers?

One of the more powerful ideas behind capitalism is *property rights*. For people to venture out to create goods and services, they must have a way to protect their rights and ideas. Think how easy it would be to make money if you could just create computers and stamp the Apple logo on it or hack into Microsoft Word and sell it at a fraction of the cost. If it was that easy to steal ideas, it wouldn't pay to create ideas. Instead, everyone would sit around waiting for someone else's idea to take off and then steal it. Everyone would realize there's no benefit in taking the risk to start a business, so no one would create. That doesn't sound like a good way to produce the millions of goods and services a nation needs.

However, if the entrepreneur can trademark the name of his campus beer store so that nobody can steal it, and if he can have a contract saying he has sole rights to his space, he may be willing to take the risk and enter into business. But who's going to enforce those rights?

Property rights enforcement is one of the key roles of government. Every nation needs to have some way to enforce property rights. How do you know you own your home? Because there's a deed stamped at the county courthouse. Nobody can dispute it. We have a central governing body that declares the rules, and the rules say it's yours. Without a governing body, someone could bully you out of your home and claim it's his. Without a government, people wouldn't go into business, and you wouldn't buy a house.

Despite the protections surrounding property ownership, some goods and services will never come into existence under a free market. For those, a government must provide what we need. What kinds of goods am I talking about?

Two Basic Characteristics of Goods and Services

You probably never thought much about it, but all goods and services have two basic characteristics. First, some goods are *used up* when consumed. If students buy a case of beer at Campus Brew and drink it at a party, once the cans are empty, it's gone. "Used up" also applies when a person's use simply keeps another from using it. If you buy a laptop computer, it doesn't get used up in the same sense as a case of beer, but you're keeping another person from using it. When you buy a computer, you've taken it out of the world's inventory of computers.

Second, some goods are *excludable*, which means they can be controlled so that others are prevented from getting them. Campus Brew, for example, has full control over its inventory and prices. The owner can set a price so that only so many are served; he can close the doors for the day; or he can simply not sell to you. The owner has total control over who gets the use of his products, within the limits of the law. (For instance, there are laws preventing Campus Brew from selling to those under the age of 21. But even here, black markets can be formed to dodge those rules.)

The private market is great at providing goods and services that fit into both categories: those that can be used up and are also excludable. Select nearly any business you can think of and you'll see that both conditions are met: the business can exclude people from using its products or services, and the goods are used up.

Common Resources and Uncommon Results

Not all resources fit both definitions. Think about fish in the ocean. They're a resource. When you catch one, no one else can catch it (assuming you don't catch and release). That resource is used up. However, can you stop other people from fishing in the ocean? Who owns the fish?

Fish are called a *common resource*; they can get used up, but you can't exclude people from getting to them. There are no boundaries or ways for people to buy property rights to the fish. And even if a system was developed, you couldn't keep fish from swimming in or out of your territory. The ocean is just too big to control the resources, so there's no way to exclude others from using them.

In these cases, we need a government to control the amount of fishing and other ocean resources so they aren't used up. While Mother Nature will replenish fish, she needs time to do it. If you just turned everyone loose to dive for lobsters in the Florida Keys without any way to control the allocation, we could "use up" the lobster population, which would become extinct.

Each lobster that's caught provides a benefit, or maybe a profit, to that person. People would overuse that resource because there's no way to set a price on lobsters while they're in the ocean. Nobody owns them. Because of the impossibility of controlling who gets them, you can't dole out property rights. If you could, the problem would be solved. Price would dictate who gets them, and the property owners (lobster fishermen) would have a strong incentive not to overfish and thus destroy their inventory.

To save these common resources, governments may limit the use by only allowing fishing at certain times of the year. They may also require licenses, which is a way of putting a price on the resources. Lobster diving may be something fun to do on the weekend, but if you had to buy an expensive license or were limited to the number you could catch, you may decide to do something else.

But when there's no price, each person has the incentive to act in his own best interest, and that's contrary to the best interest of society. Without a government to control the resources and set regulations, people would have every incentive to continue fishing. Nearly everyone else would be left with fewer fish to consume, but would not be compensated for the loss.

Economists have long known the incentive to overuse common resources. It's sometimes called the Tragedy of the Commons. An example of this happened during the Medieval Period, when shepherds had nearly unlimited land for their sheep to graze. Each additional sheep added to the flock didn't really make a difference in the amount of grass available, so shepherds had the incentive to continue growing their flocks. As shepherds acted in their best interests, the number of sheep grew, but the amount of land didn't. It became overgrazed, and the sheep population dwindled. A once thriving industry ended up destroyed.

What caused the tragedy? Each additional sheep provided benefits to the shepherd, but collectively, all became worse off. Each shepherd acting in his own best interest ended up depleting the green pastures.

The problem is that social and private incentives are different. Socially, it's best to preserve the grass and control the sheep population; individually, it's best to use the grass for your maximum benefit and increase the population. But no shepherd will take it upon himself to do what's best for the community. There's no incentive.

When Europeans came to North America, the Native Americans lived off the land and hunted wild game, such as buffalo. Europeans hunted many animals to extinction or near extinction and completely changed the way of life for the largely nomadic natives. The introduction of property rights for land and the lack of property rights for hunting not only harmed animal populations but also native populations.

A similar problem exists in Africa where many animals, especially the elephant and rhinoceros, are in danger of extinction from hunting. While it's illegal to hunt these animals, it's difficult to enforce, just as it is with fish in the ocean. Poachers have the incentive to hunt because there's a lot of money to be made. But because they don't incur any costs, it's just free money to them, and it's a race to see who can hunt the most, the fastest. They don't have the incentive to stop. If they do, another poacher will thank them for leaving more elephants and continue to hunt anyway.

However, some African countries, such as Botswana and Zimbabwe, allow citizens to own elephants—even to hunt them—provided it's on private property. The government is granting property rights to land and to the animals. Now that people can own the resources for profit, they have a powerful incentive to breed and protect. As many nations outlaw the sale of ivory, the black market pushes supply underground, and it becomes unprofitable to raise elephants and rhinoceroses to harvest their tusks and horns, and thus we actually have fewer of these animals. So, while it may seem that the profit motive is a terrible system and will quickly eliminate elephants, just the opposite is true.

After all, profits were the reason more cobras were bred in India, and profits will do the same for elephants. Profits ensure that people will use resources efficiently. It's a difficult story to tell, but as you understand more about economics, you'll see that it's the best way to make use of scarce resources.

Even Aristotle knew the problem with common resources: "What is common to many is taken least care of, for all men have greater regard for what is their own than for what they possess in common with others." It's difficult to control common resources, and for those times, governments can improve the allocation of scarce resources.

Public Goods and the Free-Rider Problem

There's another type of resource called *public goods*. These are resources that can't get used up, and you also can't keep people from using them. Though an aging example, a lighthouse is a public good. It sends a bright beam to ship captains to alert them of dangerous coastlines. If one person owns the lighthouse, he can't prevent others from seeing it. One sea captain's use doesn't prevent another from seeing it either. Whether one person sees the beam or thousands do, it's the same beam with each rotation of the beacon.

Why would any entrepreneur build lighthouses and try to charge fees for their use? They wouldn't, since people can't be prevented from seeing it. Lighthouses are a good idea for society—the benefits outweigh the costs—but the free market would never bring them into existence. This is called the free-rider problem: if a few are willing to take out memberships in a private lighthouse, most everyone else will figure out it's not worth it to pay and just enjoy the "free ride."

So we need a government to provide public goods. Military protection is one of the best examples of a public good. If citizens could elect to pay for military protection, most would choose not to enroll. Once a military is in place, everyone benefits but the armed forces can't fly over the nation and see who has a membership and who doesn't. If everyone benefits, then it makes sense that everyone should pay. The only way to have a military is to have it controlled by the government and paid for through taxes.

A government can make outcomes more efficient for public goods. Again, these are things we need, or at least we feel the benefits outweigh the costs. Governments maintain military forces to protect citizens from outside forces and provide police protection for domestic safety. These services would never come into existence if left up to the free market because of the free-rider problem.

Consider a simple example with a condominium complex. If tenants want a security guard station to monitor traffic going in and out, the management company can't just ask people to send money for its construction and upkeep. They'd end up with the free-rider problem. Everyone would figure out it's best for personal finances not to send money but still receive the benefits if others decide to create one. A guard station would never come into existence.

Instead, it's best to realize that once a guard is in place, everyone benefits, so it makes sense to have tenants vote for the service. If the majority votes yes, management can assess all tenants and put the security guard station in place. The management company is just a conduit for the tenants. It isn't a magical entity that can create a guard station for free. It taxes the tenants through HOA (Home Owner Association) dues and provides the service that the free market wouldn't have.

Condominium managers (or governments) can't create things from nothing. If a condo complex's monthly dues include cable, electricity, and Internet, does it come for free? Or does the management just assess each tenant for the cost and provide the services with that money? The problem with "package deals" is that every tenant gets exactly the same thing in the same amounts, which is probably not what individual owners would have chosen on their own. Choosing an association (or government) to provide services the free market can easily provide is inefficient.

A government does the same thing, just on a bigger scale. The government taxes citizens to provide common services (it also takes a very big chunk of your tax dollars to pay for administration). One hotly debated service is socialized medicine and Obamacare. Without even considering some of the more integral details of Obamacare, the free-rider problem alone makes it impossible for the government to provide better medical care than the private sector or to do it for less cost.

If there's a needed good or service, but no way to attach a property right to it, the free market will not provide it. In these cases, the government can possibly solve the problem, but just because the government is in a better position to solve the problem doesn't necessarily mean that it will be successful. It's usually only for public goods that the government may improve outcomes and allocate scarce resources more efficiently.

We need a government for enforcing property rights and providing military and police protection. A case could be made for the government to provide basic services such as medicine, food, and education for children, but for most other goods and services, the free market is more efficient at providing them.

What Is Government?

Just like sex, government tends to captivate some while others just ignore it. When analyzing the economics of governments and policies, realize that governments are nothing but a collection of citizens voted into office. They provide a channel to deliver certain goods and services that the free market would probably never provide or would provide inefficiently.

Unfortunately, people often feel that government is an all-knowing, superior entity that can do no wrong. Many think government has an unlimited amount of money and can simply fix problems just because it's "the government." If jobs are not being created, let the government provide them. If people aren't making enough money, let the government force businesses to pay more. If medical costs are soaring, let the government provide it for free, right?

People believe the government can just push a magic button and the problems are solved. However, if you remember that the government is just a collection of people from the nation, you'll see that those elected individuals are usually no better at solving problems than the free market.

If healthcare costs are out of control, the government still must buy those goods and services, which it does by taxing the people. But then it must decide the best way to allocate those scarce resources, and that's an impossible task. How could the government possibly know who needs what and how much?

Trying to get the government to solve these problems means a large portion of the taxes raised to get those goods and services ends up supporting governmental administration cost. Although it may seem like we're getting "cheap" or "free" healthcare, we end up spending more and receiving less.

Whenever we have what appears to be a market failure, people turn to the government for solutions. Anytime the government tries to tweak prices to make things fair, you can be sure that each citizen will respond in her own best interest, and everyone ends up worse off.

Let's explore this further by looking at the economics of taxes.

Who Really Pays the Tax?

When the economy is doing poorly, as has been largely the case since the Great Recession, citizens turn to the government for help. And government turns to business. Why not get corporations to pay higher taxes so the poor working people at the bottom of the ladder can have more money? It seems like a simple solution until you consider the economics of the idea.

Businesses, just like governments, are only collections of people who come together to create goods and services more efficiently. Imagine the thousands of things in your local grocery store. What if you had to buy each one separately from local farmers and manufacturers? It would take months to get a shopping cart full of the things you can pick up in one trip to the grocery store (or with a few clicks online).

Businesses can also make more efficient use of contracts, labor, and taxes. But remember, in the end, a business is nothing more than a collection of people providing goods and services. Therefore, taxing a business is just taxing people. Taxing a business is no way of getting money from an opulent office building; it can't pay taxes. The company logo can't pay either, but the people running the business can. Saying that the taxes came from a business may sound like you're getting money for nothing or from the multibillion-dollar conglomerate that easily has the money to pay. But, make no mistake about it, taxes are coming from people.

Are we better off taxing these behemoths to make it easier on the local citizens? If Walmart pays higher taxes, it simply taxes people in return, which it does in one of two ways. First, it can increase store prices. Walmart may be the one that sends the government a check, but the money came from the shoppers. Walmart doesn't care if the government taxes you directly or taxes the company, which in turn taxes the shoppers.

Second, if Walmart doesn't want to increase store prices, it must get the money for increased taxes from somewhere else. Just as with supporting higher minimum wages, businesses may respond by cutting wages, shareholder dividends, or workers' hours. Again, people end up paying the tax.

When politicians say they're increasing corporate taxes, it's an easy shield because they can make it sound like "evil" corporations are going to pay more money into government coffers and good, hardworking citizens are going to pay less, but ultimately any additional taxations are borne by *all citizens*. Asking the government to increase corporate tax rates is exactly the same thing as asking the government to increase prices. In short, taxing businesses can have perverse effects—another unintended consequence.

Let's say that people push for the government to raise taxes for the local yacht manufacturer. It's making multimillion-dollar products, so let the rich snobs pay the taxes since they can afford it, right? That way, the poor yacht factory workers can earn more money and have a higher standard of living.

Well, those rich folks have choices too and will respond to the newly created higher prices. Yachts are luxury items, not necessities. It's easy to just not make a purchase. Conversely, wealthy people could simply move to another brand of yacht. If all yacht brands are taxed, the rich folks could instead switch and spend that money on a new private jet, a second or third home, or any number of other things they can afford. Sales at the yacht factory would decline, and the low-income factory workers would end up bearing the brunt of the tax by working fewer hours, receiving less pay, and facing layoffs.

So, as we've seen so many times before, changing prices creates different incentives, and people respond to those incentives. Asking the government to tax corporations rather than individuals could actually have a more profound effect on your income than a direct tax increase.

The government tried this in 1990. It placed a luxury tax on things like yachts, private jets, and expensive cars. While the public cheered the decision, everyone quickly realized that it backfired, and the low-income workers bore the burden. It didn't take long for the economics of taxes to show up, and the law was repealed just three years later.

Economist Milton Friedman was in favor of eliminating corporate taxes so that governments couldn't create the illusion of taxing businesses rather than the citizens. But no politician wants to be the one who apparently favors big business over the hardworking wage earners. Once again, we realize that it's easy to overlook the details we can't see. There really is no such thing as taxing a business. You can only tax people.

Economists are usually opposed to government regulations that aren't necessary for efficient allocation of common resources. Asking the government to heavily tax corporations over the people isn't a basic need for government. Instead, it creates a platform for politicians to say they're here to help.

Save Us from Greedy Corporations

Every state has its share of natural disasters. From floods in Texas, to California's earthquakes and Florida's hurricanes, it always seems that the greedy capitalists take advantage by jacking up prices right at the time of need. It seems totally unfair that Home Depot is allowed to raise prices just because a hurricane is on its way, right?

To non-economists, the reason seems obvious: the store didn't incur increased costs, so the retailer is obviously just jacking up prices to take advantage of everyone in dire need. It's time to get the government involved to make things fair. And the government responds. Most states have "price-gouging" laws that usually say something like "stores can't increase their prices by more than 10% of the average 30-day prices during an emergency." If the average price of batteries is $5 per pack over the past month, no store can charge more than $5.50 during times of dire need.

It seems the government has helped citizens by ensuring that everyone will be able to buy necessary items like water, batteries, wood for boarding up windows, and other such goods when disaster is about to strike. But what do price-gouging laws really do? If a hurricane is approaching, people's demand for batteries increases dramatically. People are *willing* to pay more because they recognize that batteries now have more value. In this circumstance, batteries aren't for getting the TV remote to work again or operating the aquarium light. Instead, batteries may save lives as people are able to tune into a weather radio when the electricity is knocked out, or use a flashlight in pitch-black conditions when searching for food or trying to avoid a fall. The value of batteries rises dramatically when they're needed for higher-valued uses during a weather emergency. How much would you be willing to pay for batteries if they were to save your life? Certainly, far more than $5 per package.

When natural disasters are on their way, demand increases—a lot. As we found in chapter 4, an increase in demand means the demand curve shifts upward to the right and makes the new equilibrium at a higher price. For example, prior to the hurricane warning, perhaps 60% of the families in the community wanted five packs of batteries at $5 each. But with the impending danger, nearly 100% of the people now want ten packs each. However, only enough batteries were produced to fulfill the usual demand, so there simply aren't enough batteries to go around. We have a shortage. The best way to alleviate the shortage is to allow prices to rise sharply. If prices are high, people respond and only buy batteries for their most-valued use: to save life.

The government, however, won't allow it, so battery prices stay low. As we found in chapter 4, when price is below equilibrium, we end up with a shortage. With battery prices relatively cheap, people respond and buy more. If you're willing to pay $30 and the price is $5, batteries appear really, really cheap. Maybe you should buy extras. Maybe you'll buy more so you can hang flashlights in every corner of the house and have full-time light. How about some more to operate electronic games for entertainment? Why not buy lots of extras just in case this hurricane lasts an entire month? People buy lots of batteries for all kinds of uses because they're cheap, thanks to the government.

Think back to chapter 4 where the farmer had five sacks of grain. His fist sack was for survival and carried the most value. But as additional grain came into production, he valued the sacks less and less. He used the fifth sack to feed pigeons—an act significantly less valuable than saving his life. That's exactly what happens with batteries when prices are too low. Rather than buying batteries to sustain life, people can afford to use batteries for frivolous things; that is, they can afford to "feed the pigeons."

That's okay when batteries are plentiful, but certainly not fair when a hurricane is about to strike. People, however, respond to incentives, and if the price is artificially low, people will buy more than what they need for the coming emergency. When you go to the store, you'll probably find the shelves are stripped clean, not just of batteries but also of food, water, and other necessities. That's because the market wasn't able to do its job and adjust prices to regulate the instantly increased demand.

If batteries had been priced at $20, for instance, people would have the incentive to buy only what they needed. They'd realize it's not worth it to have backups or to operate electronic games. In doing so, the hot commodity of batteries stays on the shelf for everyone.

While it seems like the government is making things fair by imposing price-gouging laws and ensuring everyone has a chance to buy cheap batteries, it has the opposite effect. The laws nearly always ensure that most people go without. At super cheap prices, people buy batteries for all sorts of needs that may arise, and that's why others can't get any.

What about the people who simply can't afford batteries at such a high price? That's a problem too. But it can easily be solved by allowing the government to distribute them through certain shelters where people can prove their need. It makes absolutely no sense to keep battery prices low for everyone so that a small fraction of the population can afford them.

Running out of Gas

Many of us have seen the reports before or after a hurricane, but if you've lived through one, or another natural disaster, you know it's not just batteries that become impossible to find. Because gas prices are also forced to be artificially low, we get hoarders, rather than people buying just what they need to get through the storm. People show up with flat-bed trailers with 100 or more empty gas cans and fill them all up. They want to ensure they can run generators for months to operate stoves, lights, and all other conveniences should the hurricane hit or a little snow or ice fall in a winter storm.

Unless you're one of the first people in the five-mile-long lines that form, you're going to be left without gasoline. Even if you do decide to wait in line, you must factor in the opportunity cost of waiting. Sure, you may buy gas at $3 per gallon when you'd be willing to pay much more, but if you had to take the day off work to wait in line, you'll end up on the losing end of the deal. And if the station runs out when it's your turn to get cheap gas, you'll lose again.

Price-gouging laws ensure that most people get none while a few lucky people will have lobster tails cooking over an electric grill, with pool lights on for atmosphere, while watching movies on Netflix.

Life isn't so bad for a few people during a storm when prices are cheap. But don't overlook the things you can't see. Tens of thousands face near-death experiences because they couldn't get any gasoline. That's not a fair system, but it's how things turn out when the government tries to make markets fair—by assuming we can have it all.

Black and Gray

Price is not the only way to ration scarce goods. Why can't the government ration gasoline? Let's keep it cheap, but only allow a limited amount, say 10 gallons per family. This is the "fair" solution that non-economists often suggest. That way, everybody gets some, and the greedy capitalists don't get to profit from the upcoming disaster.

But it doesn't take much thought to realize this is a terribly inefficient idea. What if one family has three cars, all filled with gas, and doesn't foresee needing any? Another family owns one car that's running on fumes. They'd pay a lot to have 20 gallons. Well, if the government hands out rationing coupons, the family that desperately needs some will go knocking on doors trying to find someone to sell their coupons. That, however, is a terribly slow and inefficient way for the market to figure out who needs gasoline and how much.

Alternatively, the family that doesn't need any realizes the coupon could be worth a great deal to a family that does. It wouldn't take long before you'd see people offering their coupons for sale. In today's world, you'd surely find them listed on eBay or Craigslist. It's not illegal to sell them in these open markets, but they're not the intended use of the coupons either. An unauthorized or unintended market is called a *gray market*.

While the government's actions may seem like it made things fair, several problems arise. First, the gasoline market doesn't get to see prices, so sellers can't react to where gasoline is needed most. We don't know how much gas is really worth because the additional value we should be seeing at the pump is hiding in an alternative market. If gas prices could rise, sellers would respond and ship more gas to the local areas where it's needed most—the places where prices are highest. People who don't need the coupons are benefitting at the expense of the sellers who could ship more gas.

Second, people are now burdened with higher search costs. Who knows what a coupon's really worth? Some are selling for $20, others for $30, and others still higher. Potential buyers must search through all the listings to find the cheapest one and then arrange for timely and expensive delivery. After accounting for time and shipping, people would have been better off with higher prices at the pump.

Using rationing coupons is a terribly inefficient way to get scarce gasoline into the hands of those who need it most. If the free market could respond and increase prices at the pump, everyone would immediately know the prices, exactly where to find it, and could choose to buy or not.

Another problem arises with coupons. Sellers would realize that gas prices should be a lot higher, so they'd have the incentive to sell gas illegally. Illegal channels for goods and services are called the black market. Sellers would understand they could make a lot of money by selling to people who desperately need gasoline. Station owners would have the incentive to hang "no gas" signs by the road and instead profit nicely from selling gas "under the table" because of the government's good-willed intentions.

You can't stop economic forces. Governments can create policies or laws, but people get to respond. When sellers sense that prices are too low, they'll find alternative ways to sell their goods.

Gresham's Law: Where Are All the Gold and Silver Coins?

Shortages and black markets appear anytime price is below the perceived value. Throughout history, the United States had used gold and silver to create coins. The government fixed the face values at various increments, such as $1 or $10, for example. However, once the commodity value of gold increased beyond the face value, people stopped spending the coins and instead hoarded them.

If gold is worth $1,000 per ounce, but the government says the 1-ounce coin can only be used for $10 worth of goods or services, what would you do? It's not hard to figure out that people will melt the coin and sell the gold for $1,000.

The US silver dollar met the same fate. The Spanish 8 Reales was similar in size, but slightly heavier, yet the government pegged the US silver dollar as being equal to one Spanish 8 Reales. People exported the US coins overseas, exchanged them for Spanish 8 Reales, melted the coins, and sold the silver on the open market. The difference created a profit.

In 1806, Thomas Jefferson ended the production of silver dollars when he realized they were just being exported outside the country. While government officials observed the behavior, economists would have predicted it. *Gresham's Law* is an economic principle that says "bad money drives out good." In other words, if metal coins have a higher commodity value than their face value (good money), they'll be hoarded and driven out of circulation. Only the cheaper coins or paper versions (bad money) will be left as currency.

This is essentially what happens with price-gouging laws. If gasoline is perceived to be worth $5 per gallon, but the government says it can't be sold for more than its current price of $3, the high-valued uses drive out the cheaper ones. If people are willing to pay $5 per gallon, why would store owners sell it for $3? Just as silver dollars found their way overseas, the expensive gas will find its way into the hands of those who value it most.

Government regulations are becoming an increasing burden on society. The government pries into every corner of the market, trying to efficiently allocate scarce resources. Throughout history, it's a system that has been proven not to work. Yet people feel that capitalism and free markets are doomed. Ask why then does the United States produce so many goods and services and offer such a high standard of living to citizens?

Unless government regulations are properly used to allocate scarce common resources, they're going to result in inefficient allocations, and we'll end up worse off.

The Role of Speculators

All free markets have speculators, which are people willing to buy things today in anticipation of increased future prices. When I worked on a trading floor and managed an energy trading portfolio, I did this all the time. I still do it when I trade equities and options.

During housing booms, people often buy homes with the intention of "flipping" them quickly for a fast profit. Those are speculators.

Well, price-gouging laws start another set of wheels in motion. People respond to the lower prices by buying more than they need, but you'll also invite speculators who will buy things in anticipation of selling them for far greater prices.

People view speculators as greedy capitalists—let's just call them vultures—taking advantage of desperate conditions. However, they fill an important economic function: they buy when goods are plentiful but perceived to be in short future supply. Speculators pull larger supplies from the market today and bring them to market in the future, when they're needed most. Profits provide the motive.

Price-gouging laws create ideal breeding grounds for speculators. If a hurricane is coming and batteries are priced well below their perceived value, speculators will buy hundreds of packages in anticipation of selling them on street corners for nice profits.

In an active market, where prices can float freely, the speculators' actions will push prices higher. Because of the price-gouging laws, however, prices aren't allowed to move. So if one person walks in to buy hundreds of packs of batteries, the price remains the same. Why is it okay for speculators to grab all the goods off the shelf and charge higher prices to others? Why should the looming disaster provide business opportunities for individuals? One person (the speculator) racks up a nice profit, but tens of thousands of people incur much greater search costs in trying to locate the goods.

Markets will always equalize. If the government allows artificial shortages by keeping prices low, you can be sure speculators will step in and push prices back up. And it's not just government that breeds speculators. Earlier we talked about ticket prices for Jimmy Buffett concerts. It's not uncommon for major concerts or sports events to sell out of tickets quickly, only to have scalpers sell thousands of tickets on Craigslist, eBay, and in the parking lot during the event. The point is that if the government isn't going to allow stores to raise prices or if the NFL doesn't allow teams to charge more money for games, speculators will gladly accept the profits instead.

When the market is not efficiently priced, local citizens must hunt through city streets searching for a speculator to provide the higher-priced goods.

Wouldn't it be easier if you knew you could find batteries—even at higher prices—at Home Depot? During hurricanes, you'll also find that stores quickly sell out of generators. At the relatively low prices, people buy several so they can provide electricity to their entire house, including high-energy uses like the stove and refrigerator. While everyone else is left without power, for a select few, life goes on uninterrupted.

However, you'll also see parking lots with semi-trucks with speculators from neighboring states providing generators at 50% markups or more. You'll also see those in the path of the storm standing in line, gladly paying the price. Why is it bad if one person offers a product at one price, another accepts, and both are happy? Isn't that what markets are all about? People don't see it that way, though, because they don't understand how free markets work. They see it as people taking advantage of others.

But aren't the speculators taking risks when they buy hundreds of generators and drive them into the eye of the storm *hoping* to sell them? There are no guarantees. Their decision is nothing more than a short-term business venture that arises during a time of need. If products are brought when you need them most, then that's exactly what the market is designed to do. Why should anyone complain? Nobody's forcing anyone to buy. The speculators just risked their own money to help others. Yes, profit was the motive, but without that motive, no generators would appear.

Remember too that nobody has the incentive to price things higher than the market will bear. That means everyone who bought one was willing to pay the price. It would not be in the speculators' best interest to buy 100 generators and only sell 10. It also wouldn't be good to bring 100, sell out, and still have people standing in line. The speculators price generators so that everyone who wants one at that price can get one. There are no surpluses or shortages when goods are priced correctly.

So again, how can anyone say the arrangement is bad if two people agree to transact at a certain price? It takes two to tango. I am describing simple, commonsense supply and demand, just as we discussed in chapter 4. There wouldn't be any problem with this system except that the government has decided, through price-gouging laws, that it has the right to decide what price is the best to pay. These laws prevent stores with much bigger purchasing power and market knowledge to raise prices to bring those goods to market when they're needed most.

While people think the government has stepped in to make things fair and save the consumer from greedy capitalists, price-gouging laws simply create wonderful markets for speculators. Local citizens still end up paying a higher price, but now must try to locate the goods by driving around in dangerous conditions searching for those semi-trucks in deserted parking lots. It would have been much easier to drive to Home Depot where people would logically think to look.

Price-gouging laws just ensure that most people go without—even though they would have been willing to pay for the goods—while a few speculators make money, all because the government has created artificially low prices. Governments have certain roles, but trying to figure out the fair price of something is an act far beyond its ability. As long as people fail to understand the economics of free markets, the nation will always struggle with inefficient outcomes and shortages of scarce resources.

Imports and Job Protection

Regardless of the industry, people love to protect their jobs. Workers want to protect their wages; supervisors want to protect their salaries. It's a common theme as it seems reasonable that everyone benefits when jobs are protected. But remember, prosperity is not created from jobs. We can create all the jobs we want. Instead, prosperity is created from producing more goods and services.

However, because it's easy to believe that jobs are what matter, it's also easy to persuade the public that government protection is necessary. Just as people pursue their separate interests, so do government officials. They get elected by getting onto the political soapbox and saying the public needs government support to protect jobs.

While job protection is common in all industries, it's most prevalent in the auto industry. It's easy for the industry to beg for the government's help because it's such a big market that everyone understands. Just think of all the cars sold each year, and what would happen if all those employees lost their jobs. It certainly seems like it would be detrimental to the economy.

In actuality, whether it's harmful or not depends on *why* employees lose their jobs. If it's due to a falling economy, there's no argument that lost jobs are going to add to the economic drain. However, if the US auto industry is shedding jobs because they're producing autos with prices, designs, models, or quality that Americans don't want, then it doesn't necessarily mean we're worse off.

With more countries producing cars to import into America, Americans are getting cheaper cars and more selection, and that's an entirely different story. We shouldn't block imports if they benefit most Americans, even though it may be at the expense of the auto workers, an extremely small percent of the population. Everyone matters equally, and there's no reason to do the opposite: create a big benefit for a few at the expense of many.

Convincing the population that auto workers need government support is an easy story for auto workers to sell. It's easy to see all the US-made cars sitting at dealerships while the imports are flying off the lots. But it's even easier to forget about the things you can't see.

If we pay more for cars, we have less money for other things. Remember, we're always better off with more goods and services. That's the definition of prosperity. When the auto industry asks for government help to limit imports, what it's really asking is for citizens to pay more for cars. Without understanding economics, it's easy for the industry to create smoke and mirrors by showing how its workers are worse off because of cheaper imports.

Quotas and Tariffs

One of the hot buttons of the international trade discussion is that of free and fair trade, as we've discussed. Though the American model of capitalism and open trade is far from perfect, it's often much more liberal than that of many of our trade partners, who use quotas and/or tariffs on goods we import into their countries. This becomes a war cry for politicians, hence the term "trade war," which you may have heard or read about.

If the government intervenes and creates limits on the number of imports, it's usually done in one of two ways: quotas or tariffs. A quota is a regulation-based approach that limits the number of imports allowed into a country during a given time, say one year. Tariffs are a market-based approach that slap a big tax on the import to discourage sales. It's as if the government is saying, "We don't like you selling your stuff here, but as long as we get a piece of it, it's okay." With tariffs, there's no limit to the number a country can sell; instead, it must pay a tax on each item sold. The tax makes the imports more expensive and therefore less competitive.

In the end, both approaches can accomplish the same goal: fewer foreign goods are sold, thus making domestic products more attractive. The big difference is that the government receives taxes by using tariffs and gets nothing if it uses quotas. Let's take a closer look at each, but as we'll see, both approaches often backfire because people get to respond to incentives.

Quotas: The Art of Killing Competition

If the US auto industry complains that it can't compete with foreign car prices, it's not a sign of danger to the economy. It's the industry's admission that it's not as efficient at producing cars as the competition. If other countries are more efficient, we should buy from them.

If no quotas are imposed, the entire world is allowed to sell cars to America. We'd have a large supply to choose from. We'd get better choices in both price and quality. We'd have no dangers of shortages, since the entire world can supply more cars than America could ever desire over any given time. The only companies that could compete are those able to offer lower prices or better quality, which means consumers benefit.

But what happens if the government imposes a quota? We end up with fewer imports, and therefore the supply of cars declines and car prices must rise in response. There's no question that rising car prices benefits US auto workers—exactly what that industry seeks when requesting the government's help.

Focusing on benefits alone, however, is a dangerous way to allocate scarce resources. What about the costs? Auto workers account for a very small fraction of America's economy. But by having every single citizen pay more for cars, we're doing more harm than good. We end up with a small percentage of the population that benefits, but the vast majority have huge costs imposed in the form of higher car prices. Citizens have less money with which to buy other goods and services. Those goods never get produced, and corporate sales suffer because people are using more money to buy higher-priced American cars.

Anytime you hear an industry stage a campaign to "Buy American" or limit the number of imports, they're simply asking citizens to pay higher prices for their goods. That's never a beneficial result because we end up with fewer goods and services.

So the question then becomes, does anything good come from trade restrictions? Not usually, because people—and countries—respond to incentives. The country that's reducing the imports will usually face retaliatory tactics from its trading partners. The United States may end up importing fewer Toyotas from Japan, but we'll also end up exporting fewer Fords to them. What the US auto workers gain from blocked foreign imports may very well be more than lost by fewer exports of their goods.

These tactics aren't necessarily retaliatory, however. Japan pays for its US imports through the sale of its exports. When the United States prevents Japan from selling here, it's the same thing as asking Japan to buy less from us. By limiting Japanese imports, we're giving them fewer dollars to buy from us.

Of course, what the auto workers are hoping for is that Japan buys just as many US cars, but in reality it reduces Japan's purchases of other US goods, perhaps boats. If that happens, are we really better off if we sell $100 million dollars more of American cars but have $100 million less in boat sales? The auto workers never show that hidden side of the equation because it's always easy to overlook things that aren't produced.

Still, sometimes countries will enter into *voluntary export restraints* if one complains that its domestic industries are seeking protection. These self-imposed restrictions are done to pacify the importing country so that retaliatory tactics are not used against the trading partner. Are we better off under those conditions?

If you said yes, you're forgetting that people respond to incentives. In the early 1980s, the United States faced stiff competition from Japan, and auto workers begged for the government to intervene. Japan entered into a voluntary restraint agreement, but it created different incentives. Toyota created Lexus, a whole new higher-end brand that did not directly compete with the low-end market that the United States auto manufacturers were lobbying against. Other Japanese manufacturers followed. Nissan developed Infiniti, and Honda produced Acura. These cars gave Americans more choices, which further hurt the US auto industry.

To makes things worse for auto workers of domestic manufacturers, these Japanese manufacturers opened US factories to produce their cars domestically. By trying to reduce foreign competition, the regulations actually increased it.

Does that mean we're worse off? Not at all. We now have more auto factories that employ US citizens, and competition has produced better cars. It's a perfect example of how productivity creates jobs. It shouldn't matter which cars we're producing. Instead, we should focus on who is producing cars most efficiently. If a country can produce cars more efficiently, we should buy from them and use the extra cash for other goods and services.

Imports don't harm jobs, they just shift the factories people are working in. Should citizens work for the factory that manufactures cars efficiently or inefficiently? It's a simple question that's easily masked by shifting the focus on job protection. The US auto workers may not be too efficient at producing cars, but they're very good at producing reasons why they need protection.

Tariffs: The Art of Killing Competition —for a Fee

Tariffs are designed to do the same thing as quotas, but they approach it from a price standpoint rather than trying to limit the actual numbers.

With tariffs, the government doesn't impose restrictions on the number of goods sold. Instead, it imposes a stiff tax. The higher price reduces foreign sales, which means there are more US sales made to make up the shortfall. The government also receives money from the taxes.

From both of those perspectives, the United States benefits. But at the higher prices, consumers miss out on the opportunity to buy cheaper foreign goods. Since US manufacturers are more expensive, consumers buy less than they would if they could purchase cheaper foreign goods. Overall, the US economy still has a net loss.

People protecting jobs is nothing new. The word *sabotage* comes from 15th-century Netherlands when angry workers threw their wooden shoes, called *sabots*, into the gears of the new textile looms. Workers feared the automated technology would put them out of work, so they set out to destroy the malicious machinery that would surely destroy the economy.

Were they right? Just think how much worse off we'd be today if all our bedsheets were still woven by hand. We'd have very scarce—and expensive—sheets, and we'd have far more workers used to create the same amount of linens. When I ran my company making custom bedsheets, one of the very reasons the company never took off is that the volume was so low that the high cost of handmaking the product prevented us from getting orders big enough to justify manufacturing large quantities.

Without technology and progress, we'd need most of the nation's labor just to produce textiles. If you're still thinking it would've been better if all the textile workers could have kept their jobs, you've fallen for the easiest trap in economics: overlooking the things not produced. Had that many workers been kept in the textile industry, they couldn't have eventually moved on to work in the production of cars, computers, or other things we now find more valuable.

The 15th- century textile looms did destroy a small number of jobs, but progress gave rise to massive industries that created far more jobs than the new technology destroyed. And many of those who lost their low-paying jobs were able to move into higher-level management jobs in the textile factories.

It's easy to see these advantages of the new looms now, looking back. But fast forward 600 years to the 21st century, and people still face the same fears when it comes to improved technology—or competing countries—that can produce things for less money. While we may not throw shoes into machinery, we create the same effect on a larger scale by throwing the government into the intricate gears of the market. We hope to make things fair, but we end up sabotaging the very system that provides the benefits we seek.

The Iowa Car Crop

There's nothing like a good parable to shed light on economic mysteries. The Iowa Car Crop is one such story, outlined by economist Steven Landsburg in *The Armchair Economist*.

The tale tells of a fantasy machine, located in the Pacific Ocean, that transforms wheat into cars. Of course, something this great could never happen; it would be too good to be true. But if such a machine could be invented, would you vote for lawmakers to use it? Of course you would! Being able to exchange wheat for cars, who wouldn't vote for that? Think how much better off we'd be with such a machine. It's almost like getting cars for nothing. Well, we do have a "machine" that can do that: Japan.

When you understand economics, you'll see we have two ways to make cars. The first is the traditional way in which we employ engineers and mechanics in Detroit. The second way is to employ farmers in Iowa to make wheat that transforms into cars. Let me explain: the farmer grows wheat and sends it overseas to Japan. Japan, in return, either pays for the wheat in cash, or it can trade it for cars. If farmers feel they're getting a better deal by accepting the cars, they'll act in their best interest and do so.

Japan may pay $10 million for the wheat, or it may offer to trade $12 million worth of Toyotas that cost far less than $10 million to produce. If the farmers accept, everybody wins. From the Iowa farmers' perspective, they received $12 million in goods (Toyotas) for only $10 million worth of wheat. Japan received $10 million worth of goods (wheat) by paying less, perhaps just $8 million worth of inputs to build the $12 million worth of Toyotas. Everybody's better off.

The farmers ship the cars back to the United States, where they are sold, which means the farmers essentially created cars from wheat. There's absolutely no difference in the result if the farmers had instead dumped wheat into a machine that created cars. Driving through Iowa, it's easy to see wheat crops, but it takes an economist to see the car crops.

Notice, however, that when the problem is worded as "international trade"— Japan exporting cars to the United States—it's easy to believe the Detroit auto workers were harmed and the nation is worse off. There's no question that Detroit workers were financially harmed, but it's not true that the nation is worse off.

The amount of financial damage done to the auto workers was more than offset by financial gains to farmers and, in turn, financial gains to citizens who can buy cheaper cars. Overall, the economy is better off.

The benefits are overlooked because people never realize that farmers are in the auto business—and so is everybody else who exports to Japan. Nike can ship clothing to the same machine and bring back Toyotas or Sony televisions, Nikon cameras or Kawasaki jet skis.

If the government steps in to protect the auto workers in Detroit, it's a policy that unfairly favors them over the farmers in Iowa. Detroit may scream for the government to save them from foreign competition, but that foreign competition is not really Japan. Its farmers and other businesses right here in the United States.

Don't get me wrong. As I have said, I am a car guy. I love all those old Jeeps made in Toledo and cars from Detroit, but why is it fair for Detroit and Toledo to get protection just because their workers can scream louder than the farmers in Indiana and Kansas? It isn't, of course!

If a country has many ways for producing cars, it should use all methods in ways that maximize value for all citizens. Remember the farmer with five bags of grain? He used the bags in accordance to their values: the highest-value bag to feed his family, the lowest-value bag to feed pigeons. That's how we should treat auto production. Use your most efficient ways first, and then move toward the less efficient ways as more supply is needed.

Farmers will only continue to ship wheat in exchange for cars as long as it's profitable. If Detroit produces cars more efficiently, it will eventually cut into the farmers' profits, and they'll stop. The market will take care of the process all by itself—if prices and competition are allowed to float freely. If instead the government steps in and forces one of the production methods to stop, US citizens must then pay more for cars.

If that's hard to understand, think about your household. You have lots of choices for transportation. You can travel by foot, bike, car, or airplane. If you're free to choose, you'll find the right mix for your needs. You may walk to the mailbox, ride your bike to the corner coffee shop, drive your car across town, and take an airplane across the country. But how would you feel if the government forced you to choose just one method of transportation? Would you be better off? It would be unbearably inefficient and expensive to choose just one method for all needs. Yet that's exactly what happens when the government forces everyone to buy from Detroit.

By blocking foreign imports, our government takes away the alternative methods of production—such as farmers—that may be more efficient for some of the cars. You wouldn't be better off if you could only choose one form of travel, and the United States isn't better off by having all cars produced in one place. When Detroit pushes to be the sole car producer, it gains at the expense of farmers and citizens who now must pay more for transportation.

When you hear the media heat up with "Buy American" campaigns, be careful about the policies you vote for. A car manufactured in Detroit is American, but so is one grown in Iowa or my home state of Indiana.

Making Rent Prices Fair

One of the most visible areas of government price controls is in rents. When apartment prices get "too high," consumers beg the government to do something to make them fair. Consumers don't understand that the high prices are a reflection of the many people competing for limited housing. Instead, they see it as landlords taking advantage of tenants.

If the government passes a rent-control law, it puts a limit on the amount apartment owners can charge per month. For example, a landlord may be able to rent an apartment for $1,000 per month, but the government may say he can only charge tenants $600.

Now think about the newly created incentives to tenants and landlords. Tenants are buyers, and the Law of Demand says that more people will buy when prices are low. Well, that's exactly what happens. More people move to the city to take advantage of the lower prices. Other people, who may not even need an apartment, could decide to rent one just because they can. Why not have an extra place for the weekend if the price is right? The lower prices create a big wave of people who weren't there before, all looking for apartments. But the supply of apartments hasn't changed.

Landlords respond too. At lower prices, entrepreneurs aren't inclined to build apartments. Why would anyone want to invest his hard-earned money on an investment that doesn't pay? Might as well take your money elsewhere. If instead rents could float when more people move to the city, prices would rise and more apartments would be built in response to the higher prices. But when the prices are low, nobody has the incentive to put their money into an apartment and rent it out for next to nothing.

You must always remember the reason we have goods and services; it's because people are responding to incentives. Just as we found that McDonald's and Walmart don't exist because they owe people jobs, apartments don't exist because landlords owe people places to live. They're businesses. If you wouldn't use hundreds of thousands of dollars of your own money to buy a rental property because you'd get nothing in return except constant headaches and repairs, don't expect anybody else to do it either.

With rent control, landlords and builders will respond in one of three ways. First, those currently in the market will pack up and take their money somewhere else. Second, no new landlords or builders will enter the market and build new apartments. Third, the few remaining landlords will recognize that if the market wants $600 worth of apartment, then that's what they'll provide. In other words, don't expect a whole lot for your money. Landlords will cut corners. Tenants will find broken windows, shoddy air conditioning, leaky pipes, and lengthy delays when repairs are needed.

This is exactly why you'll find the worst housing conditions wherever there are rent controls. It's also exactly why you'll see more homeless people on the streets. Low housing prices attracts lots of people, but it doesn't give investors/landlords the incentive to provide.

What's a better way to handle the housing shortage? Let prices float freely. If many people wish to move to the area, prices will rise in the short run. But as prices rise, people respond to the incentives. You'll see new home builders entering the market and many entrepreneurs putting up their money to become landlords. The additional supply will eventually bring housing prices back down, but with many more new apartments in the area.

If prices are apparently too high, what can be done? Well, people may have to get roommates or accept smaller apartments. But this is exactly where the problems are for most Americans. People expect that they should have a large, two-bedroom apartment just for themselves. They don't realize it's a matter of scarcity. There just aren't enough apartments to handle all the demand for housing.

There's no question the nation will always have some people who truly cannot make ends meet. And there are ways to provide for those people. But that's an extremely small segment of society. For them, it makes far more sense to have government-subsidized housing or tax credits, for example, rather than making prices artificially low for *every single person* who could otherwise afford it. When the government creates artificially low prices for everyone, it ends up squeezing out the very people who need it most.

Propping up Stock Prices

Price controls aren't just for the United States. In June 2015, China's stock market peaked, with the Shanghai Composite Index topping out at 5,166—an increase of 150% over the previous 12 months. It then began a precipitous plunge, with the index falling to 3,507 in less than a month—a 32% drop—shaving off $3 trillion in values.

Rather than letting the market do its job and find the collective opinion of stock prices, the Chinese government attempted to artificially prop up prices. It changed many of the market regulations, including postponing initial public offerings (IPOs), threatening to imprison short sellers, requiring the national pension fund to purchase equities, and banning all major shareholders, directors, supervisors, and senior management from selling any shares.

China's central bank cut interest rates to a record low and provided nearly $20 billion worth of its currency to buy distressed stocks. Companies could also choose to suspend their shares so that investors couldn't buy or sell; 50% of the shares were blocked at one point. Overall, the government created 40 new regulations to keep its market from melting down.

The market clawed its way back and rallied 13% to 3,965, but this was an artificial climb. Trying to force the market to balance at a contrived price level never works. It just postpones the inevitable and usually makes the final outcome worse.

When governments make desperate moves like this, investors realize they're not looking at true market valuations. Nobody has confidence in the market prices as they know they're artificially high, so investors act in their best interests and sell while they still can. The market falls faster and harder—just at a later date. Tweaking prices is a dangerous tactic, and history has shown us that in the long run these strategies simply cannot and do not work.

Agricultural Subsidies

Governments across the globe engage in farming subsidies. Some are good. Some not so much, such as when a government guarantees a certain price per bushel for the production of a given crop. For example, a government may guarantee $3 per bushel for all corn produced over the next year. Regardless of the subsidy amount, the idea is to ensure that farmers can earn enough money from their crops to continue producing food for the nation.

The problem is, with guaranteed prices, farmers have an incentive to produce far more of the subsidized crops than would otherwise be done under a free market—just like the cobras of India. Subsidies often create overproduction. When all farmers show up to market with a huge supply, prices plummet, which can drive out smaller farmers, thus giving pricing control to the bigger farms.

Further, if farmers are paid a guaranteed amount, they have an incentive to quit growing other crops which may be subjected to price risk. Instead, they use that land to grow more of the crop that comes with a promised profit. Thus, all of the farmers' benefits come at the taxpayers' expense.

When prices are artificially high, people go into overdrive to produce things the market doesn't need. When one industry cries for government regulations to keep prices high to preserve jobs, it may save a few, but as you can see, it can create far more expenses in the process.

The Role of Government Regulations

Government regulations are necessary for running an economy. But the government's scope should be limited to things the free market may not provide, such as allocating common resources, enforcing property rights, and protecting citizens from inside and outside forces.

Today, people seek more and more government regulations to make things "fair." The government responds. After all, if citizens are asking for more of its services, it will gladly oblige. But if people wouldn't vote for policies that would allow the government to decide whom you should date or marry, you have to wonder why people want the government to make equally intrusive regulations that have no bearing on private matters.

For instance, in Minnesota, local governments require a vendor license if you want to sell pumpkins and Christmas trees. In Texas, you must have a license to be an interior designer, and Wisconsin requires a license if you wish to go out of business. We've all heard about Mayor Bloomberg's New York ban on businesses selling sodas larger than 16 ounces, which was eventually overturned by the state's Supreme Court. Judge Milton Tingling said that Bloomberg's attempt at "portion control" was both arbitrary and capricious. Well said. I hope you're starting to think like an economist: don't forget to think about the things you can't see.

Uber is benefiting people all over the world—even in my small Indiana town. The company's gross worldwide booking for 2016 was more than $20 billion, and despite losing $2.8 billion in 2016, investors are confident that the ridesharing and ride-hauling business model will turn large profits in the future.

Sure, Uber is lowering traditional taxi drivers' income, but far more people will have incomes rise because they're spending less on taxis. That extra income ends up in the pockets of other American businesses, so it's completely false to say that Uber harms businesses. To the contrary, it's making travel more efficient and is therefore contributing to productivity.

It shouldn't be up to the government to decide who gets to drive you from one place to another. As we have learned previously, it is also not the government's job to bail out Uber and save all the driving jobs if the company has to declare bankruptcy. These are just a few examples that prove false the belief that government must play an ever-increasing role in making private decisions for citizens.

If you want to hire someone as a cab driver or an interior designer, it should be your choice. Both of you can easily agree on a price, and you'll end up being better off. You shouldn't need the government's seal of approval for that transaction. The government didn't sign off on artist Pablo Picasso, singer Michael Jackson, magicians Penn and Teller, or Chef Wolfgang Puck (though my taste would prefer touring diners, drive-ins, and dives with Guy Fieri in his Camaro). These are all various forms of art, and it's best to leave it up to the public to decide who's worth the price.

On the flipside, regulation that keeps known felons from driving for Uber or child-molesting interior designers from entering your home would be worthy interventions the government might possibly make. Requiring needless licenses or other types of intervention are all forms of price control. By limiting the number of taxis, for example, the price of their services will be higher.

The basic idea behind capitalism is to have a free market, one where individuals can make their own decisions. But when the government intervenes, it's forcing you to make choices it wants you to make. That's not freedom. In contrast, it's the first step toward bigger government, more intrusions, and inefficient allocations of scarce resources.

Economists know price controls rarely work. In the words of economist Milton Friedman, "Economists may not know much, but they do know how to produce a shortage or surplus." All that needs to be done is for the government to create artificially low or high prices. So the next time you hear that the government will artificially raise or lower prices, it's not a sure sign of prosperity. It's a guaranteed sign of an upcoming surplus or shortage.

Remember, it takes two to tango, and when the supply line and the demand line come together to dance, it creates equilibrium. Surplus or shortage, it doesn't matter—both are bad.

If you hear minimum wages will be raised artificially high in your area, don't thank the government for handing you more money. Thank your employer for handing over your last check. And if you hear prices will be kept artificially low during a looming natural disaster, don't be the first to cheer the government's actions. Be the first to the store to stock up before it's all gone (or, better yet, buy the entire inventory and sell it on the corner to all the others willing to pay any price).

CHAPTER 7

SPECIALIZATION AND THE GAINS FROM TRADE

W hy are economists in favor of international trade when businesses and employees all seek government protection from imports? Why do nations trade with each other if citizens believe they're worse off? Like most economic puzzles, it's a matter of accounting for the things you can't see. And when it comes to economics, there's probably no bigger misunderstanding than the benefits of trade.

You may not realize it, but every day everyone is engaged in trade, and everybody benefits. Trade isn't just for big-ticket items like the Iowa Car Crop we talked about in the previous chapter. Trade is all around us.

Consider the labor market. You may not think of this as a market for trade, but it certainly is. When you go to work, you're trading hours of labor in exchange for cash. The employer is trading cash in exchange for your labor. Both parties feel they're better off, otherwise they wouldn't be doing it.

The benefit of trade arises when you have a large supply of something. Because the product is so abundant, it has a low value to you. You can trade some of that product (or resource, such as labor) with another person who has a low supply and therefore values it highly. From your perspective, you're exchanging something of low value for something that has much higher value. It's a big benefit to you. If it's advantageous to you, why would the other person engage in trade with you? That's the magic of trade: each party has exactly the opposite problem; they are in short supply of what's in high supply for the other.

Consider our farmer, with his five bags of grain. With so much grain, the fifth bag doesn't have much value to him, so he uses it to feed the pigeons. However, let's say he has no water. A neighbor happens to own a well. Just like the grain farmer, the neighbor will value water less the more he has. He may reserve one gallon for survival. He may use the second gallon for basic health and hydration. He may use the third gallon for watering the plants, and so on. In fact, he has so much water, he uses the next gallon to fill bird baths for the pigeons. But he has no food. It's easy to see how both people could swap grain and water to become better off. Each person gains life-saving benefits at nearly no cost.

That's really the essence of the benefits of trade. Just swap things that are in high supply (and have low value to you) in exchange for things that are in short supply (and have high value to you). Each person benefits because each sees the other person's inventory as more valuable. Once you understand the advantages of trade on a small scale, it's not difficult to understand them on a larger scale.

Florida Oranges for Georgia Peaches

Just as two people can benefit from trade, so can two states. Florida gains advantages by trading oranges for peaches with Georgia. Oranges are plentiful in Florida, so they have relatively low value there. Georgia has lots of peaches, so they see peaches as having relatively low value. Florida would like to have peaches, and Georgia would like to have oranges. So the former values peaches highly, while the latter values oranges highly.

How can both states become better off? Each state can exchange what it produces for something the other produces. Florida thinks it's gaining by trading low-valued oranges for high-valued peaches. Georgia sees the exchange in the opposite way: it's trading low-valued peaches for high-valued oranges. Both states are happy and in a better position from the exchange.

So what's the problem? If you don't consider the details, it's easy to see why Florida's orange grove employees will say the imported peaches are destroying their jobs. If the industry seeks government support to ban imported peaches, then we're right back to the Iowa Car Crop, just using different products.

Enacting laws to benefit Florida's orange growers creates equal harm to Florida's grapefruit growers, for example, since they could ship grapefruit to Georgia and bring back peaches in exchange. If all people matter equally, protecting orange growers is exactly the same thing as imposing punishments of equal size on grapefruit growers.

Trading Beyond Borders

If it makes sense for two people to trade or for Florida to trade with Georgia, it should make equally good sense for the United States to trade with China, Mexico, or Canada. After all, what difference does it make where the borders lie? As long as both parties benefit, there's no reason the government should ban exchanges. Each country always has advantages in what it can produce. It may have more natural resources, more high-skilled or low-skilled labor, or more technology than another country.

Let's say the United States is more productive at brewing beer, while France is better at making wine. By "better," we mean the country can produce it at a lower cost. Another way to say it is that for the same amount of resources (land, labor, capital), one country can produce more than the other.

Assume that during one day, the United States can produce 75 cases of beer while France can make 20 cases of beer. France, on the other hand, can make 100 cases of wine while the United States can only produce 25 cases of wine:

	Beer	**Wine**
U.S.	75	25
France	20	100

Notice that the United States is more productive in beer (75 cases versus 20 cases) while France is more productive in wine (100 cases versus 25 cases). When one country is more productive with a particular good, it has an absolute advantage. In our example, the United States has an *absolute advantage* in beer production, while France has an absolute advantage in wine production.

As with all economic transactions, there's a tradeoff. If the United States decides to spend the day making 75 cases of beer, it "costs" 25 cases of wine. In other words, during a 24-hour period, the United States can produce 75 cases of beer or 25 cases of wine. If it chooses to use all its resources for making beer, it can't also use them for producing wine. To make 75 cases of beer means the United States must sacrifice 25 cases of wine. Therefore, to make one case of beer costs 1/3 of a case of wine.

If the United States decided instead to make 25 cases of wine, it gives up 75 cases of beer. Therefore, one case of wine costs three cases of beer. France has different ratios. To produce 20 cases of beer, it must give up 100 cases of wine, which means one case of beer costs five cases of wine. If France wants to make 100 cases of wine, it gives up 20 cases of beer, so one case of wine costs 1/5 of a case of beer.

Can the United States and France become better off by trading with each other? At the end of the 24-hour production day, if both countries can wind up with more than they could on their own, the answer is yes. But how should the terms of trade be set? Take a look at the costs of beer and wine for each country:

	Cost per Case of Beer	**Cost per Case of Wine**
U.S.	1/3 case of wine	3 cases of beer
France	5 cases of wine	1/5 case of beer

Notice that beer is relatively cheap for the United States to make because it only gives up 1/3 of a case of wine while France gives up five cases when making beer. This may seem confusing, but just think of these numbers as a form of payment. We can pay for beer with wine, but we could also pay for it with money. Would you rather pay $5 for beer (like France) or 1/3 of a dollar (like the United States)? Obviously, 1/3 of a dollar is cheaper. In other words, the United States sacrifices less wine to produce beer, which means the United States is more efficient at producing beer.

Now look at the cost of wine. The United States gives up three cases of beer to make wine, while France gives up 1/5 of a case of beer to make wine. The United States would "spend" a lot of beer to make wine. France only "spends" 1/5 of a case of beer, so it's far cheaper for France to produce wine.

If you were a world manager running beer and wine production, which country would you appoint to make beer and which to make wine? Its common sense: select the one that produces each product the cheapest. The United States should specialize in beer while France specializes in wine. By specializing in respective strengths, each country can trade with the other and end up better off. Each could agree, for example, to trade four cases of beer for one case of wine:

1 case of beer = 4 cases of wine

The United States previously had to give up three cases of beer to gain one case of wine, but under the terms of trade, the United States can now get four cases of wine. If the United States spends its day making 75 cases of beer, it can exchange four of those cases with France and gain one case of wine. At the end of the day, the United States has 71 cases of beer and one case of wine—something that was impossible to do on its own.

With trade the United States has beer plus an extra case of wine at the end of the day because beer is cheaper for it to produce and wine is cheaper for France. France is also better off because it can get beer cheaper. France used to give up five cases of wine to get one case of beer. Under the new terms of trade, France can make five cases of wine, exchange one, and get four cases of beer. France has wine and beer, which is something it wasn't able to do before trading, at least not during the same 24-hour period. Countries are always better off by trading with each other for the simple fact that each country has different resources and different costs of production.

The Hidden Benefits of Comparative Advantages

However, what if one country is better—has an absolute advantage—at making *both* goods? It doesn't matter. Any two countries can benefit from trade, regardless of where absolute advantages may lie. That's because it's not only the country that can produce at the cheapest cost, it can also be the country that produces at the cheapest opportunity cost.

Let's create new numbers and assume the United States can produce more beer or wine in a day:

	Beer	Wine
U.S.	50	150
France	5	25

It may seem there's no reason for the United States to trade with France since it can produce more of both goods in a day. Why trade with a country that's less efficient at producing goods?

But notice the United States is 10 times more productive in making beer (50 cases of beer versus France's five cases of beer) but only six times more productive in wine (150 vs. 25). Relatively speaking, France is better at producing wine. In other words, even though the United States can produce more of both goods, France's strength lies in wine. Think of it as France is "less bad" in the production of wine compared to beer, so it has a relative advantage in the former. This is called a comparative advantage.

The interesting thing about comparative advantages is that if one country has an absolute advantage in two goods, the other country mathematically must have a comparative advantage in one of them. This is why any country can always gain from trade, even if it's better and more efficient at producing all goods.

In this example, if the United States produces 50 cases of beer, it must give up 150 cases of wine. That means one case of beer costs three cases of wine. If

France produces five cases of beer, it must give up 25 cases of wine. In other words, one case of beer costs five cases of wine:

United States: 1 case of beer = 3 cases of wine
France: 1 case of beer = 5 cases of wine

Just as before, rather than thinking of wine as the price, think of these goods in terms of dollars. Which is cheaper: $3 for one beer or $5? $3 is a cheaper price, so therefore three cases of wine is a cheaper price compared to five cases of wine. That means the United States produces beer at a cheaper cost because it gives up less wine.

Both countries can benefit by specializing in the goods where they have a comparative advantage and then trading with another country for goods in which the other has a comparative advantage. Both countries can benefit by finding some ratio between three cases of wine and five cases of wine. For instance, perhaps both countries agree to exchange one case of beer for four cases of wine:

1 case of beer = 4 cases of wine

Prior to opening up trade, the United States had to give up one case of beer to produce only three cases of wine. After agreeing to trade with France, the United States can now produce one case of beer and exchange it for four cases of wine. The United States gains one case of wine. It's as if we're back in biblical times and wine is magically produced out of water.

How does France gain? Prior to trade, France had to give up five cases of wine to produce one case of beer. But after agreeing to trade with the United States, France can produce five cases of wine, but only exchange four cases of wine with the United States for one case of beer. France has also created a free case of wine.

In this example, the numbers were contrived so that beer costs the United States exactly three cases of wine and exactly one case of wine for France. Both countries benefitted by agreeing to trade a case of beer for four cases of wine—exactly halfway between three and five.

In actuality, any "price" or number that falls between the two opportunity costs of three and five would work too. Both countries could have also agreed to trade one case of beer for 3.5 cases of wine, 4.7 cases of wine, or any number between three and five. The only time trade doesn't work is if the ratios for both countries are the same for both goods or services. For instance, assume the following numbers instead:

	Beer	**Wine**
U.S.	50	100
France	5	10

Here, the United States is 10 times better at producing beer and 10 times better at producing wine. The two countries can't benefit from trade. In the real world, the chances of both countries having identical ratios is virtually zero. And even if the ratios were identical, they can't be identical for all goods and services that both countries produce, so again *all* can benefit from trade.

Specialization Is Key

Once you understand how two countries can benefit from trade, you'll see why it's best for people to specialize and trade with others. This is why, for example, a doctor may be able to type more words than a secretary but still decide to hire one. The doctor has a high opportunity cost for typing because he must forego surgeries or office visits to type emails and invoices. If a doctor can earn thousands of dollars per hour doing surgery, it becomes very expensive to type.

A secretary, on the other hand, will be comparatively better at typing since the opportunity costs are lower. A secretary may only be able to earn $15 per hour in a particular field. Because of the high opportunity costs, however, a doctor may be willing to pay $30 per hour to have someone do his typing. By trading typing for surgery, the doctor and secretary are better off. Notice how easy it is to overlook the benefits of trade. That's because they're difficult to see.

It's much easier for certain industries to say we can't compete with China because of its low labor costs. But remember, the very benefit of trade stems from one country having some type of advantage. If China has extremely cheap labor compared to the United States, it's the perfect setup for beneficial trade.

Unfortunately, it's usually used as the perfect setup for government intervention to protect US jobs. But by understanding trade, you can see that such interference doesn't help. Instead, it forces the United States to have fewer goods and services, which is to say, we're not as wealthy.

Remember, wealth is not created from jobs; it's created from productivity. Let the most productive country specialize in what it does comparatively best and trade with other countries that are comparatively better in other things. Everyone ends up with more goods and services. Everyone is wealthier.

One of the companies I owned throughout the years was a plumbing business. It was my best venture, and looking back, it would have been the most profitable of all my entrepreneurial endeavors if I'd stayed with it.

Billy, a licensed master plumber, worked for me. One afternoon he came back with a check for $95, our standard service call fee. He'd just been to the home of a female attorney. Her toilet wasn't working. He rang the bell, greeted the woman politely, and after about four minutes in the bathroom, he had the problem fixed. He took another minute to write an invoice and then presented the homeowner with the invoice.

The attorney refused to pay the $95 fee. She complained that it was highway robbery—even *she* didn't charge $95 for five minutes of work. Billy told her that it was no problem. He'd be glad to go back into her bathroom and return the toilet to how it was before he fixed it. Needless to say, she gave Billy $95.

To make the most of your career, spend your time specializing in valued goods or services. It may seem like you're saving money by trying to do everything yourself, but you must consider the opportunity costs of your time. It may only take Billy four minutes to fix your toilet, but how many hours and trips to the hardware store would it take you?

Even if the government occasionally blocks the benefits of trade, don't take that as a sign of protection. It's a sign of politics getting in the way of progress.

CHAPTER 8

MONEY AND INFLATION

Money may not buy happiness, but it does make it easier to be miserable. We all know what money is. It's the green stuff everybody wants. It's the reason we work. But if money is just pieces of paper, why do we need it?

Through the centuries, money has appeared in every civilization. It can be anything generally accepted as payment. I'm talking cattle to cowry shells. It's all been used throughout history as currency. Commodities such as gold and silver have also been popular.

Money serves three basic functions:

- It's a medium of exchange
- It's a unit of account
- It's a store of value

Let's look at each of these in turn.

Medium of Exchange

The first reason for having a currency is that it allows for more efficient exchanges of goods and services. In the absence of money, people resort to barter: I'll trade you my pizza for your case of beer.

Barter, however, is extremely inefficient because to get what you want, you first have to find someone who has what you want. And then you must hope the person is willing to trade it for what you're offering. In economics, that's called a *double coincidence of wants*. In other words, two people have to find each other and have exactly what the other one wants. If you have a case of beer and want a pizza, you have to spend a lot of time searching for someone who has a pizza and is looking to exchange it for a case of beer.

That problem, however, goes away when you have a standard currency. If you have a case of beer, you might sell it for $20 to someone who wants beer. It doesn't matter if that person is willing to trade a pizza. You have cash, and it acts like a token, showing you've produced $20 worth of goods and services. You can take that cash and exchange it for anything you want. If you decide to buy a pizza, effectively you've traded beer for pizza, but you did it more efficiently.

The person who bought your beer may not know how to make pizza—but he did want your beer. Rather than spending your time searching for someone with a pizza who's willing to trade for beer, you just sell the beer and buy the pizza somewhere else.

So why does the pizzeria accept your $20 bill? For the same reason you accepted the $20 cash for selling your beer. The pizzeria owner can take the cash and buy whatever he wants. Maybe he buys more flour to make pizza dough for his business. Maybe he hires someone to mow his grass. It doesn't matter, and he's free to choose whatever he wants in exchange for that pizza.

Currency acts like a sophisticated accounting tool. It keeps tabs on the value of what each person has produced. If you don't produce anything, you don't sell anything, and you can't buy anything.

Currency allows for the most efficient distribution of goods and services, and that's why any modern society will always have a currency. There has to be a way to account for who is producing stuff and who is buying stuff. The only way you can buy $20 worth of goods is to produce that same amount.

As the economy expands, people are better off because they're all producing things other people want and exchanging the money for things they want. Even though you've heard the expression "Money makes the world go round," it's really production that makes the world turn. When people produce, economies expand. Money just makes production more efficient.

Unit of Account

The second benefit of a currency is that it provides a unit of account, which just means that money allows people to have a consistent way to measure value. When all goods and services are priced in dollars, it's easy to see relative values. You just need to know what everything is worth in dollars.

If a pizza costs $20 and a case of beer also costs $20, you immediately know that one pizza can be exchanged for one case of beer. If a bottle of wine costs $40, it's easy to see that two pizzas can be exchanged for one bottle of wine. While it seems like a simple idea, simple comparisons like this get complicated in a barter economy.

If an economy has just five goods, you'd need 10 different prices to conduct business. How many pizzas can be exchanged for beer? How much beer for wine? How much wine for peanuts? The list gets out of control quickly since it grows exponentially: with 20 goods, you'd need 190 different prices; for 100 goods, you'd need 4,950 prices. You can only imagine the number of prices you'd need for the millions of goods and services we have available. It would be impossible to run an economy efficiently by trying to figure out what each product or service is worth compared to all the others.

Not only is it terribly inefficient, but it's nearly impossible to tell the relative prices of goods. Which item is more expensive? If you can exchange one pizza for one case of beer, one pizza for 20 bags of peanuts, 40 bags of peanuts for one bottle of wine, and three bags of pretzels for one bag of peanuts, how many cases of beer can you exchange for pretzels? Confusing, right?! And that's just a handful of goods. Imagine if you had millions of goods and services.

That problem, however, goes away when you have a currency. When everything is priced in dollars, you have a single measuring stick, one unit of account. You just need to know how many dollars it takes for each product or service. When you hear the price in dollars, it's easy to see what each is worth relative to others. If you know beer costs $20 per case and pretzels cost $1 per bag, then it's easy to see that 20 bags of pretzels are equivalent to one case of beer.

Store of Value

The third function of money is that it allows you to defer purchases. You may decide to produce and sell something today, but you're not required to exchange it for something else immediately, as you must in a barter economy. With currency, you can save the cash and convert it to goods in the future. In other words, money allows you to store value.

The ability to store value also helps to manage risk across time. If you don't need things today, you can hang on to the cash. If you do need things today but haven't produced anything to sell, you can use your saved cash to buy what you need. Cash allows you to smooth out needs and manage the risk of surpluses or gluts over time.

But don't forget there are problems with money. To have the economy run smoothly, there has to be enough money in the system to allow people to exchange it for things. Think of a small island with $100,000 worth of goods and services available. If the economy only has $100 floating around, it's not doing much good. People can't get their hands on the cash to engage in transactions. It's too rare relative to the amount of goods available, and islanders will resort to barter to carry out most of their transactions. Money loses its usefulness.

To solve this problem, early economies turned to naturally existing things, like cattle and cowry shells. In ancient times, salt was used to pay the Roman legions, which is where the word *salary* is derived from, along with the expression to be "worth your salt." Salt had tremendous value at that time because it allowed people to preserve food.

The problem, however, is that if someone stumbled onto a huge pile of shells or a big salt mine, he'd be instantly wealthy. There would also be a huge increase in the amount of "money" relative to the goods. With more "money" in the economy, it may seem that everyone would be better off. How could more money be a bad thing? Yet a problem does occur when there isn't an equivalent number of goods produced, as when a bunch of money just appears.

When there's a huge increase in the amount of money, you get a wealth effect and things suddenly appear cheaper. People want more goods because they have the money to buy it. However, if there's only more money without a corresponding increase in the number of goods, people compete for the limited products or services by bidding prices higher, just like the folks before a hurricane who want a generator. If there's only one case of beer, but a whole lot of new people have gone to the store to buy it, everyone realizes they must bid higher.

Based on the Law of Demand, what happens when there's a shortage? Prices rise. And that's exactly what happens when there's newly found money. There's a relative shortage of goods, and prices rise. In economics, that rise in prices is called inflation. But what exactly is inflation, how is it caused, and why is it a problem?

The Ravages of Inflation

President Reagan said, "Inflation is as violent as a mugger, as frightening as an armed robber, and as deadly as a hit man." Economist Milton Friedman said inflation is taxation without representation. Whatever you call it, inflation is a serious threat to your investments and future financial decisions.

Inflation is the general rise in prices. It's hard not to notice that prices rise just a bit each year. For the United States, a $1 soda may cost a few cents more next year, and a $40,000 car may cost an extra $1,000. It's like there's a small current pulling prices higher.

It's not unusual to hear people explain this as the direct result of capitalism. They believe business owners tack on profit each year, which drives up the costs for producers, who in turn have to jack up their prices. Capitalism, however, tends to keep prices down because of competition. Inflation is caused for a different reason, and that reason is the government printing money.

Most modern currency is called *fiat money*, which means it has no intrinsic value like coins made of gold or silver do. Instead, it's just declared by the government to be legal for all public and private debts. Fiat money has value only because people believe it will continue to have value. As long as citizens believe they can use the money to buy other goods and services or pay off debts, they're willing to accept the currency.

However, the Law of Supply shows that as the number of anything rises, its value falls. Money is no different. If the number of dollar bills circulating increases, the value of each dollar falls. Governments love to print money as a way to pay off debts. Think what you'd be tempted to do if you could print money to pay off credit cards and student loans. The prospect would be irresistible, and that's exactly why no government can say no to it. Rather than raising taxes, it just prints money, which reduces the value of everyone's money.

Inflation is really an illusion. Prices aren't really rising. Instead, the dollar's value is falling. But when the dollar's value falls, it appears that things are getting more expensive. And citizens pay the price.

If the government prints more money than the amount of goods and services produced, you'll get inflation. For the United States, the inflation rate runs about 2% to 3% per year, depending on the time span being measured. We've been much higher, pushing 15% in 1980. Like any average, you'll get fluctuations, so don't think 2% to 3% inflation means it's always in that range. That's just the long-term average.

If gross domestic product (GDP) rises by 3%, but the government prints 5% more money, you're going to get roughly 2% inflation. That's because there are more dollars floating around in the economy, but with no corresponding goods or services to purchase. The only way money can get absorbed is for prices to rise by the amount of excess dollars.

Governments resort to printing money so they can continually spend without raising taxes. It may sound like a good deal, because it appears we get more stuff without having to pay for it. But, as you know by now, there's always a tradeoff.

As long as inflation doesn't get out of control, it's not too bad of a problem. But when inflation is persistently high, it poses problems for a number of reasons.

Problem #1: Erosion of Purchasing Power

Inflation eats away at your purchasing power. If you have $10,000 in savings, it can buy $10,000 worth of goods and services today. If there's 3% inflation, however, you'll lose purchasing power. Even though you still have $10,000 cash, it will only buy about $9,700 next year. You lost $300 for doing nothing.

Inflation also harms investments. If you invest and earn 10% but inflation is 3%, you only earned the 7% difference. Even though you may have 10% more dollars, they're not worth as much, so you're effectively earning less. Three percent may not seem like a lot, but it compounds over time. If you invest $10,000 and earn 10% per year for 10 years, you'd have nearly $26,000. But if 3% inflation was present in each of those years, your money will buy just $19,700 worth of goods and services. You effectively lost 24% of your money—even though your stockpile increased from $10,000 to $26,000. Inflation is just like a thief. It's taxation without representation.

Problem #2: Future Planning Becomes Difficult

A second problem of inflation is that it makes it difficult for people to plan for the future or make future investments. How would you respond to a $50,000-per-year job? It may seem like a fair amount, but if inflation is rampant, you can't predict whether that amount will cut it. The outcome may be quite different from what you planned. It would be hard for you to accept the position without knowing the true costs. People can't make decisions effectively if they're not sure about future costs or the value of money.

The problem is compounded for bigger, longer-term projects. Imagine the difficulties in trying to plan for a large office complex or theme park. It would be nearly impossible to determine what the project is worth because the value of money is uncertain. It's safer not to undertake the project, which means productivity slows. Wealth is then decreased for everyone.

Problem #3: Price Distortion

People respond to incentives, and the price mechanism is the nation's way to determine who needs what. When prices are low, it sends a message that those resources are in high supply and don't carry much value. If prices are high, it sends a clear message to the market that we need more of those resources.

Prices work best when they're allowed to rise and fall with changing needs. However, if inflation is present, prices just generally rise, so it distorts the benefits conveyed by prices.

Problem #4: Inflation Creates Money Illusion

If prices are consistently rising, it may appear that real wages are rising, but it's just distortions with inflation. If inflation rises quickly, employees may be lured into working longer under the belief that they're better off. But if inflation is rampant, they're probably falling further and further behind with each passing year.

Inflation causes people to spend time and other resources to produce things that aren't needed. They're taking on projects because they think there's value, but it's just an illusion. The evidence clearly shows inflation is strictly due to sudden increases in the money supply. In the 1850s, the California gold rush created a rapid surge in the supply of money—and a heated round of inflation followed.

If inflation gets out of control, it's called a hyperinflation. While there's no formal definition of what constitutes hyperinflation, it's usually considered to be unusually high rates that are accelerating. If a country has 10% inflation per year, it's not hyperinflation. Rather, it becomes hyperinflation when the patterns look like 10%, 20%, 50%, 200% per year, and so on.

When hyperinflation occurs, it's usually the beginning of the end for the currency. Eventually, people will stop accepting it as a form of payment. A post-WWII example is Zimbabwe, where the government printed money hand over fist to pay off debts. Out-of-control inflation followed. It was so heated that it was nearly impossible to calculate the inflation rate. Many official reports showed inflation at more than 200 million percent *per month*. That's not a typo; it's what happens when runaway money printing occurs. The Zimbabwe central bank ended up printing a $100-trillion note. At the time, it was worth about $5.

Throughout history, Austria, China, Germany, France, Hungary, Argentina, Peru, Brazil, Czechoslovakia, and, most recently, Venezuela have experienced hyperinflation. Regardless of how long or how bad the inflation, it has always stemmed from the government printing money. There has never been a case in history where a rapid increase in the amount of money was not followed by inflation, and there has never been inflation that wasn't preceded by a rapid increase in the amount of money.

Inflation is a silent killer, which is why you must understand it—and account for it in your financial decisions.

CHAPTER 9

RECESSIONS AND DEPRESSIONS

Productivity is the key to prosperity. With more goods and services to go around, prices fall, and everyone ends up better off. But how do we know how much stuff is being produced?

For that, economists turn to GDP. In simple terms, GDP is a number that the Bureau of Economic Analysis (BEA) calculates to show the total dollar value of all *final* goods and services that have been produced in a given year. "Final" goods means finished goods, rather than intermediate goods being used in the process of making something else.

For example, if you buy a loaf of bread for one dollar, that dollar gets added to GDP. You were the final user of the loaf of bread. You weren't buying the bread as an input for making something else. However, the bakery may have purchased flour from one business and yeast from another. None of those costs get tacked onto GDP since they are incorporated into the seller's price. The final loaf of bread includes all the previous prices paid to produce it. If the price of flour and yeast had been included in GDP too, it would be like double-counting.

For 2014, the US GDP was about $17.3 trillion. That means if you took all the goods and services sold during the year, their values would add up to that total. GDP is also thought of as a reflection of the economy's health. When people produce goods and services, those sales create incomes to the sellers. So when we measure GDP, we're also measuring incomes. That's why economists like to see a steadily rising GDP. It reflects a growing economy with rising incomes.

Each year we economists want to see the GDP rise by about 2% to 3% as the economy expands and new technologies allow us to produce more things for less money. That's what creates wealth. Remember, jobs don't create wealth. Production does. That's why economists pay close attention to GDP.

The BEA reports GDP numbers each quarter. It uses an elaborate system to estimate GDP based on statistical samples. It always reports the number as annualized, so if GDP grew at 1% for the quarter, the BEA will announce the economy grew at a 4% annualized pace for the year. That doesn't mean the economy grew 4% during those three months. It means that if the economy keeps growing at its current 1% rate, it will end up being 4% at the end of the year.

People mistakenly believe that China has the largest economy. For 2014, its total GDP was about $10.4 trillion—well below the United States' $17.3 trillion. China, however, was making news because it had the fastest GDP growth rate for several years, but that doesn't mean it was producing more goods and services.

The following chart shows GDP growth for the United States since 1950:

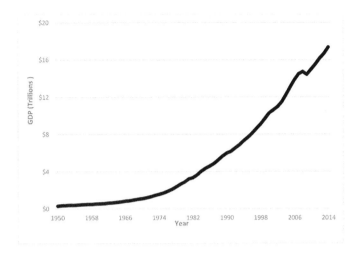

Occasionally, you may hear about gross national product, or GNP. Both GDP and GNP are related, but there's an important difference. GDP counts the value of all final goods and services produced *within* a country's borders, regardless of who owns it. For the United States, if it's manufactured inside our borders, it gets counted in GDP. For example, Nissan Motors is Japanese owned, but it maintains a factory in Tennessee. All cars produced at this factory get counted as part of US GDP.

GNP, on the other hand, only counts businesses controlled by a particular country—regardless of where the businesses are located. Exxon, for example, has oil drilling rigs in Russia, so all that production gets counted as part of US GNP, even though that production takes place outside US borders. Exxon is a US corporation, and that's all that matters for GNP.

Nominal GDP versus Real GDP

If GDP or GNP increases from one year to the next, one of two things had to occur: the United States either produced more goods and services, or it produced the same number of goods and services but sold them at higher prices.

As we discussed in the previous chapter, inflation causes prices to rise a little bit each year. If the United States reports higher GDP next year, is it because we actually produced more things? Or did GDP rise because of inflation? To account for this, economists use two different measurements: nominal GDP and real GDP.

The word *nominal* means "name," so it's the actual GDP figure reported for that year. If the United States produced $17.3 trillion worth of goods and services for 2014, then the nominal GDP is $17.3 trillion. However, the BEA tracks inflation by calculating the price for a particular basket of goods and services. It then measures the prices of those same goods and services each year. If you were able to buy the basket of goods for $100 in 2009, but that same basket cost $108.65 in 2014, then prices, on average, increased 8.65%.

To compare 2014 GDP growth to 2009, the BEA adjusts nominal GDP of $17.3 trillion by dividing by 1.0865. The adjusted GDP number is called the real GDP, which just means it's a reflection of the "real," or true, growth in goods and services. For 2014, real GDP was $15.9 trillion ($17.3 trillion/1.0865). This 1.0865 adjustment factor is called the GDP deflator since it "deflates," or reduces, GDP by the amount of inflation present during that time.

Economists are mostly concerned with real GDP since it's a reflection of the true increase in the number of goods and services produced.

Not Too Fast, Not Too Slow

There are optimal levels for most things in life. We don't want to sleep too little or too much. We don't want too much or too little rain. And just like Goldilocks, we don't want our soup too hot or too cold. We want it just right.

The economy is no different.

Ideally, we'd like to see GDP grow by about 2% to 3% per year. If it's growing slower, we can't produce the necessary goods and services for the growing labor force. We end up with high unemployment and a sluggish economy: a recession. If the economy grows faster than 3%, it's growing too quickly. Employees and equipment are pushed to the limits, and just like running a car at maximum speed, the pace can't be sustained for very long. If there's a huge demand for goods and services, but they're not getting produced fast enough, prices get pushed higher and we end up with a big round of inflation. But with GDP growing about 2% to 3% each year, the economy sustains a smooth ride.

Recession: Economic STDs

If the economy's doing well, prices generally rise as the increased demands put upward pressure on prices. This is called a *demand-pull inflation*, since it's the demand that's pulling prices higher. On the other hand, sometimes the economy can face price shocks, such as with spiking oil prices, which can increase the costs of goods and services across the board. This is a cost-push inflation because costs are pushed higher. As costs are increased, they increase the costs to others, who in turn must increase prices to cover costs.

The primary cause of long-run inflation, however, is when the government prints money to relieve its debts. If the money supply grows without an equal increase in the number of goods and services produced, it can only get absorbed into the economy through higher prices.

This is exactly why the government can't just print money to make everybody better off. If the government credited everyone's checking account with $1 million tomorrow, everyone would begin spending, but there would be no new goods and services produced to satisfy the higher demand. So people would be willing to pay more for the same amount of goods and services, and prices would rise.

Regardless of the cause of inflation, higher prices also cause other economic wheels to turn. With higher inflation, consumers' purchasing power is decreased, which simply means they can buy fewer goods and services with the same amount of money. As prices rise, interest rates will too. As the economy is humming along, people are more inclined to borrow money to buy homes, cars, and other big-ticket items. Businesses are also likely to borrow to stock up on inventory or build new offices or factories. As people compete for the limited dollars available for loans, interest rates rise.

With higher prices and interest rates, people then spend less, and businesses produce less in response. As sales slow, employees get laid off and then spend even less. As spending slows and unemployment rises, consumer confidence falls. People begin saving more and spending less as fears of layoffs increase. It becomes a vicious cycle, and the economy slowly sinks. The economy has entered a recession.

While there's no definite way to say exactly when an economy falls into recession, most economists declare it an official recession if GDP falls for two consecutive quarters. Another sign that things are overheating is when GDP is growing at rates beyond 3% per year. Numbers that high usually mean we're in a speculative bubble, and asset prices are simply being driven higher not because more things are being produced, but because of some future expectation.

A recent example is when the United States had a housing bubble from 2000 to 2008. Property prices in some areas increased 30% per year for four or five years. That means some home prices quadrupled during the eight-year period. Based on the Law of Demand, as prices rise, people buy less. So, in most cases, rising prices will temper the number of sales. However, during a speculative bubble, people expect prices to continue rising, and that changes the dynamics of supply and demand.

Each year between 2000 and 2008 that people decided not to buy a home, they regretted it more and more because prices continued to rise ever higher. This led to a further increase in demand for homes, which led to further price increases. As prices spiraled higher, people were even more convinced that prices would be still higher next year. This in turn made people demand homes even more, and the cycle continued.

Eventually, people realized that the prices had gotten out of control. It only took a few news articles showing mortgage defaults were on the rise and that property values were starting to decline. Then everyone rushed for the exits as homeowners dumped a huge supply of homes on the market, causing prices to plummet. The bubble had burst.

China is currently experiencing similar growing pains and will likely be dealing with them for years to come. Amazingly, China's government has not reported a GDP growth number below 6% since 1990. It's doing everything in its power to sustain the growth, but as you now know from reading this book, the Chinese government's artificially propping up the economy cannot end well.

Bubbles can cause prices to collapse in any industry, but they're not always devastating as they are when they threaten the financial system. For instance, if the market for rare art, gold coins, or—near and dear to my heart—collectible cars collapses, it's self-contained and just affects buyers and sellers in that market.

However, bubbles are ruinous when they undermine confidence in the financial markets as this distrust can lead to recessions or depressions.

When the housing market imploded, for instance, few people wanted to buy homes. According to the Law of Demand, as home prices fell, the lower prices would normally have led people to purchase property and so stabilize prices. However, banks also knew the market was unstable, so they didn't want to make loans. Without loans, few people were able to buy homes, so prices continued to fall. Then a bigger problem emerged.

Many homeowners had taken equity loans against their property, which is partly what helped the economy to grow so strongly in prior years. As home prices rose, equity loans almost paid themselves off by the increase in property values. But with home prices falling, equity loans got more expensive, and defaults started to make headlines. These problems trickled over to the bond markets. Investors, banks, and pension funds invest in bonds, but when the threat of default increases, the bond market dries up.

When speculative bubbles threaten the financial system, economists are especially concerned because with less money circulating, sales slump and businesses begin to lay off employees. As unemployment rates rise, employees get nervous about their future employment, so they begin to pay off loans and quit taking out new loans. This deleveraging means there's even less money in the economy, which causes sales to slump further. It becomes one big vicious circle: the economy slumps, GDP falls, and the economy enters a recession.

If the problem persists, investors can also lose confidence in the political system too. The Chinese government is particularly cautious of any kind of economic event that would cause political unrest. A sharp Chinese recession or a depression could ultimately cause a revolt against the political system, and since government officials are appointed and not elected, the very leaders working to keep stability in the economy are also fighting to keep their personal political power and wealth.

If financial investments are collapsing, nobody wants to invest. Instead, everyone wants to hoard cash in case they lose their jobs. Eventually, investors may quit buying government bonds, which means the government's revenues are reduced, and it must now pay higher interest rates to entice investors to lend money. Not only is the economy threatened, but so is the financial and political system. Nobody's buying, nobody's selling, and the economy grinds to a halt.

The biggest problem with falling GDP is that the economy can never make up for lost time. (We will discuss the same problem that individual investors face later.) No matter how much higher GDP may be in the future, the negative years always represent missing output. The nation's GDP would have been larger had it not encountered a recession.

Depression: Economic Abortion

If a recession gets too bad, the economy can sink into a depression, which is really just a severe recession. There's no clear-cut way to say if and when an economy has entered a depression, but it's usually characterized by long periods of high unemployment, say 12% or more. When the American financial system collapsed in 1929, unemployment reached 15% in 1931, peaked at 25% in 1933, and didn't fall below 10% until 1941. So, for 10 straight years, unemployment remained at double-digit levels.

The most concerning thing about recessions is that there's no reason for a recession to stop until some significant catalyst causes people's perceptions to change. The main thing that has to change is people's confidence about future progress. As long as unemployment remains high and confidence stays low, there's no reason to believe people will suddenly begin to have confidence in their future job prospects and decide to start spending again.

Businesses have no money coming in and certainly aren't going to begin producing new goods and services, hoping that they can sell them. Something has to change, but if there's no reasonable catalyst, what can we hope for? This is another case where government intervention may be warranted.

The Government Steps In: The Federal Reserve

Severe recessions or depressions often need an economic stimulus to get the economy going again. The government will often bail out banks or other financial institutions to stabilize the economy. However, if an entire financial collapse occurs, it could lead to a serious depression lasting for years.

The Federal Reserve, or Fed, is the nation's central bank. It was created by Congress in 1913 under the Federal Reserve Act. It acts as a bank's bank. If you need a loan, you go to a bank. But if a bank needs a loan, it goes to the Federal Reserve. Most nations with a well-developed capital market will have a central bank to perform similar functions.

The Fed is charged with three key goals for the nation:

- Maximize employment
- Create stable prices
- Moderate long-term interest rates

The Fed acts independently of the government but is subject to oversight by Congress. Its actions are supposed to be free from political bias because its decisions don't have to be approved by the president or any other agency.

The Fed is guided by a Board of Governors, which is made up of seven presidential appointees elected for 14-year terms. Members must be confirmed by the Senate and can be reappointed. The board is led by a chairperson and vice chairperson, which are appointed by the president and approved by the Senate for four-year terms. Janet Yellen became Fed chair in February 2014 after Ben Bernanke. Before that was Alan Greenspan, who held the seat for 19 years.

The Federal Open Market Committee (FOMC) is charged with reviewing economic conditions and making recommendations on the appropriate monetary policies to sustain the goals of high employment, long-run price stability, and economic growth. The Board of Governors members are also members of the FOMC, which is made up of 12 members. So, of the 12 members of the FOMC, seven are from the Board of Governors. The FOMC holds eight regularly scheduled meetings each year, roughly every six weeks. During these meetings, the committee reviews economic data to assess the nation's health and make recommendations for warming or cooling the economy.

The Fed has three key tools for getting the economy back on its feet (or calming growth). All three methods are indirect ways of influencing interest rates. If the economy is sluggish, the Fed may decide to lower interest rates, which encourages businesses to borrow for new factories or other investments.

It also gives consumers the incentive to buy big-ticket items, like homes, cars, and appliances. When people spend on big-ticket things, it also affects many more businesses. If housing booms, then banks, real estate agents, contractors, plumbers, electricians, surveyors, suppliers, and many others see a boost in business too. As spending increases, businesses produce more and hire more employees to meet the increased demand.

If GDP is growing too quickly and the economy is heating up, the Fed may raise interest rates to slow down spending and economic activity. Changing interest rates alters the incentives for people to spend. To keep the economy cruising along at a healthy pace, the Fed is charged with keeping interest rates at an ideal level. So how does the Fed alter interest rates? Aren't they determined by the market? Well, yes and no.

The market does ultimately determine interest rates, but the Fed can't just snap its fingers and change the interest rate. However, it can strongly influence them to move up or down to desired levels. Depending on how much of a move or how quickly it needs to be made, the Fed relies on three key tools.

Fed Tool #1: Open-Market Operations

The Fed's most popular tool for altering interest rates is the use of open-market operations. It can buy or sell bonds in the open market, and in doing so it changes the amount of dollars circulating in the banks. As the supply of dollars changes, so does the price of money—the interest rates.

If the Fed buys bonds in the open market, it spends cash, which gets deposited into banks. In other words, the Fed is able to inject surplus cash into the economy that otherwise wouldn't be there. When the supply of dollars increases at banks, they have the incentive to lower the interest rate in an attempt to lend out the excess cash.

The reverse happens if the Fed sells bonds. By selling bonds, banks spend cash and receive bonds. By spending cash, the banks have less cash, which puts upward pressure on interest rates.

Open-market operations are by far the most common way the Fed can alter the money supply to influence the direction of interest rates.

Fed Tool #2: Changing the Discount Rate

When banks need a loan, they can go to the *discount window* at the Fed, and in return they are charged the discount rate of interest. Most banks that borrow from the discount window are doing so for short periods of time, usually overnight.

If the Fed increases the discount rate, it sends a signal to banks that they're on the hunt to increase rates. Most banks, in response, will voluntarily increase rates. And if the Fed reduces the discount rate, banks will follow suit and reduce interest rates.

The big difference between open-market operations and changing the discount rate is that open-market operations will ultimately force rates lower because of the large supply of money dumped into banks. Changing the discount rate, in contrast, is a subtle way of letting banks know that rate changes are imminent, but there's no way it can force rates to change.

Fed Tool #3: Changing the Reserve Requirement

You're probably familiar with the basics of how banks make money: they entice customers to deposit money by paying interest on checking and savings accounts. Then they loan it back out to others at a higher rate. The bank may pay 2% interest for a checking account but charge 6% for a car loan and keep the difference, or *spread*, as profit.

However, you probably didn't know that banks can't loan all of that money out. If banks loaned 100% of all deposits, there'd be no money left in the banks for customers to make withdrawals. The good news for banks is that all of the customers never want all of their money all of the time. Most of it just sits idly in the account, so banks just have to keep a small fraction of all deposits in the vaults, just in case people want to make withdrawals. Because banks only keep a fraction of the total deposits, it creates what is called a fractional reserve banking system. The alternative would be a 100% requirement, or full reserve banking, but no banking system in the world requires such a strict standard.

The specifics get complicated, but generally speaking, US banks have to withhold 10% of each deposit, which is called a reserve requirement. Because banks only have to withhold a fraction of the total money deposited, it creates an expansionary process: the amount of money circulating in the economy is far greater than that issued by the central bank.

Here's how it works: if you deposit $1,000 into a bank, the bank must hold 10%, or $100, as a reserve requirement. It is allowed to loan out the remaining $900. If that bank makes a $900 loan, that money may get deposited into another bank, which in turn must withhold 10%, or $90. That bank is then allowed to loan the remaining $810. The process continues, and ultimately there will be far more money circulating in the economy than the initial $1,000 deposit.

It's easy to figure out just how much would be created. If the reserve requirement is 10%, just take 1/0.10, which equals 10. That means the amount of money is increased by a factor of 10. Your $1,000 deposit ultimately creates $10,000 of additional money circulating in the economy.

The Federal Reserve sets this minimum requirement. If it increases that number, banks have less money to lend out since they must hold more money in reserve. For instance, if the requirement is increased to 12%, the multiplier becomes 1/0.12, or 8.3 times, instead of 10. If banks have fewer dollars to lend but the amount of loans people want remains the same, there'll be a shortage of dollars. We'd have too many people demanding loans that the banks couldn't make. Banks would then have the incentive to raise interest rates to balance supply and demand.

On the other hand, if the Fed lowers the reserve requirement, it will increase the amount of money in circulation. Lowering the requirement to 8% makes the multiplier 1/0.08, or 12.5. As the amount of dollars increases, banks become flush with cash and have the incentive to lower interest rates to balance supply and demand.

While changing the reserve requirement definitely alters the supply of money, the Fed is reluctant to change these conditions because of the radical changes it can cause to the money supply. Small changes in the reserve requirement can dramatically increase or decrease the amount of money in circulation. Still, it remains a powerful tool available to the Fed in times of extreme situations.

Fractional reserve banking makes the banking system a potential house of cards. If all depositors rushed to the banks or ATMs to withdraw money, some would find no money is available. If that happens, it's called a run on the bank, which could cause a banking collapse. Once one bank fails, the word spreads, and soon other depositors are lining up at their banks to withdraw all their money before their bank fails.

Most runs on banks are purely psychological. As bank depositors hear about bank failures or see others lining up at the doors to withdraw money, it sends a signal to the rest of the economy that banks may be failing. It then becomes a self-fulfilling prophecy: banks fail because everyone thought they would and reacted accordingly.

The potential for a bank run is one of the reasons the government created the Federal Deposit Insurance Corporation (FDIC). If you have a checking or savings account at a commercial bank and the bank fails, each account is insured up to $250,000. By having this "peace of mind" guarantee, people are less likely to lose confidence in the banking system during a crisis, withdraw their money, and make things worse.

It's no accident that the FDIC was created under the Banking Act in 1933 as part of the solution for getting the economy out of the Great Depression. Since 1934, no depositor has lost money because of a bank failure. Insurance provides the incentive for people not to fear the fractional reserve banking system.

However, just because the economy may be in a slump doesn't mean the Fed will step in and decrease interest rates. Lower rates may give people the incentive to spend, but that can also send false signals through the economy. Any type of economic stimulus package can actually prolong the process of getting out of the rut. Instead, the Fed's actions should only be used in times of extreme hardship, such as 1933 and 2007. Economist John Maynard Keynes even said that when the Fed increases spending in hard times, it should be building surpluses when times are good.

Unfortunately, that never happens. Instead, governments like to use Keynes's theory as an excuse to spend continually. The Fed's actions to raise or lower rates are artificial ways to increase or decrease spending. Just as when any method is used to artificially hold prices high or low, it never works in the long run. For the Fed, altering the money supply to prompt spending will usually have bad repercussions if used for anything other than extreme recessions or depressions.

CHAPTER 10

FROM DATING TO COMMITMENT:

The Importance of Financial Decisions

Have you ever been car shopping? As we have now learned from economics, everyone is driven by incentives, and if you're in car sales, your incentive is to maximize your commission.

One of the salesman's best tactics is to find out what you can afford to pay each month to own the car. Notice that he doesn't ask you for your budget for a car, but the budget for your *payment*. The human mind has a funny way of rationalizing things, and when buying large-ticket items, the monthly payment is the guideline most people use to make credit decisions. It's also why most people end up putting themselves in dangerous financial positions. In credit and life, decisions you make today stay with you forever.

Every decision you make is a financial one. Whether you're deciding to buy stocks or bonds, watch a movie or dine out, or figure out who to date, it's ultimately a financial decision. Remember what my grandpa said: there's no free lunch. That means all decisions require good financial analysis. Because there's always a tradeoff, ask what the next best use of that time or money would have been. That's the true cost of the decision.

Let's say you're planning to buy a $25,000 car and make monthly payments on a five-year loan. At 3% interest, that's $450 per month. You may be making enough money to swing those payments, but that doesn't make it a good decision. Instead, take a different perspective—an economic one—and focus on what you're giving up. For instance, what could you have done with that money by investing in the stock market and earning some average amount, say 8% per year? If you invest $450 per month at 8% per year, you'd have over $33,000 after five years!

I am a HUGE "car guy." To say I love cars is an understatement. But I have never bought a new car, and that example is why. If you buy a new car for $25k, after five years you'll have paid over $29,000 in total. You'll own it outright, but it won't be worth much. Cars depreciate—quickly. The second you drive the car off the dealer's lot, it'll lose at least 20% of its value.

On the other hand, if you choose to invest in the markets and earn 8% each year, you'd have $33,000 in the bank. Now that you have a dollar value to compare, you can measure the tradeoff. The decision isn't whether you can afford to make the car payments; it's whether you can afford to miss out on $33,000 in five years.

Buying the car creates a loss of nearly $29,000 (your $25k car is likely to be near worthless at the end of five years). Putting those same payments to work in the market may put $33,000 in your pocket. That's the cost, but the cost doesn't end there. If you continue driving the car after it's paid off, its value continues to fall. If you'd invested instead, your returns would continue to rise. If you drive the car for another three years, your $33,000 investment will grow to nearly $42,000. Buying the car eventually leads to nearly a 100% loss, at which point you're ready to buy a new car and dig an even deeper financial hole.

Cars are far more expensive than most people realize, but that's easy to overlook since the true cost—the opportunity cost—is a cost you never see. It's not a cost you write a check for. It's an economic cost. It's the cost of a missed opportunity because you can't use the same dollars twice. You can buy the car or invest in the market—not both.

Of course, stock market investments don't allow you to get around town. Without a car, you'll have a hard time getting to work. Having to walk to work or take a bus or cab (more likely, an Uber) creates another set of opportunity costs. The efficiency of getting around town in your own car has benefits too.

If you don't want to take the risk of investing in the stock market, you could make those payments to yourself in a savings account. You won't earn as much over the long haul, but at least you'd have liquid cash to bail you out in times of an emergency. If you lose your job, that cash can support your house payments for several months while you find a new job.

Viewed in this light, choosing to buy the car increases the risk of losing your home. It doesn't matter how you choose to spend money, there's always a tradeoff because you can't spend the money twice. Now you see why any decision is never as easy as it seems. The car has costs and benefits—and so do investments. But if you at least consider the value of what you're giving up, you'll make more informed decisions.

What if you have an asset that's paid for? Are there still opportunity costs? You'll often hear retirees say their homes are paid off and therefore represent no cost. That's because they're overlooking what they're giving up. If someone owns a million-dollar home outright, there may not be a mortgage payment, but there's still a cost. The home could be sold and the money placed in a risk-free asset, such as a bank CD. If that CD is paying 3%, the free and clear million-dollar home represents a missed opportunity cost of $30,000 per year in income. By choosing to stay in the house, even though it's paid for, the owner must give up $30,000 per year. By comparing the risk-free rate, we know for sure that's an amount that could be collected each year by selling the property.

You get a choice, and you must consider the alternatives to make the best financial decisions. Always consider the opportunity costs: what could you have done with the money otherwise?

Cars represent the second largest purchase for most Americans. As I've just shown you, they have enormous opportunity costs, mostly because of how quickly they depreciate. However, the largest purchase for most is a home. Real estate represents much better assets as its price tends to rise over the long run. In response, many homebuyers try to get the most house for the smallest payment, which often leads them to choose adjustable rates over fixed-rate mortgages. It may seem like the financially prudent thing to do, but you have to understand the mechanics of how a fixed-rate mortgage works compared to adjustable rates.

Fixed-Rate versus Adjustable-Rate Mortgages

Owning a home may be the American dream, but it can quickly become a nightmare if you make bad economic decisions. Many people do—and end up losing their homes as a result.

Most people have to take out a loan to buy a house, and there are a couple of ways the banks will offer interest rate terms: fixed and adjustable. With fixed-rate mortgages, your interest rate never changes. If your mortgage rate is 3%, that rate stays exactly the same for the entire term of the loan, even if it's a 30-year mortgage. No matter how high interest rates may climb, your monthly payments are calculated at 3%.

Most banks also offer adjustable-rate mortgages (ARM), which seem attractive, especially to new homeowners. Your interest rate is tied to some base interest rate and then reset at fixed periods of time, usually each year. For example, you may pay the base rate plus 1% after the first year and the base rate plus 1.5% the next year. Every loan is different and interest rate caps may exist, so there may be a limit as to how high your rates can go, but if interest rates rise significantly, your monthly payments could more than double.

With adjustable rates, your interest rate typically starts much lower than current market rates—but only for a short time. Adjustable rates can be attractive if you know for sure that you're going to be in the home for a short time. However, this backfired in 2007, and many people got into trouble.

Prior to 2007, home prices were rising significantly, and many speculators bought homes with ARMs in an attempt to "flip" the property quickly for a nice profit. If they had understood economics, many would have been saved from financial ruin. As people were raking in money by flipping homes, others saw those profits and responded to those incentives: more people jumped into the action and pushed home prices even higher.

It's always a sure sign of a housing market bubble when you see television shows spring up like *Flip This House*, which showed viewers just how easy it was to buy homes for no money down and quickly flip them for a quick profit. At some point, however, all of those future expectations get priced into today's homes, and eventually people end up buying greatly overpriced real estate that they can't sell. Once everyone realizes they're at a market peak, they rush to sell, prices plummet, and the bubble bursts.

However, some decided not to sell when the property market began to crash in 2007 and 2008. Instead, they gambled on a quick housing-market recovery. They ended up worse off. Their adjustable rates climbed while housing prices crashed. Many ended up owing more on the homes than they were worth. They couldn't keep up with the rising interest rates and were forced out of their houses. The sure-thing speculation turned into financial catastrophes.

Many could have been saved by using fixed-rate mortgages. However, that option doesn't mean your total monthly payment can't change. With a fixed-rate mortgage, only your principal and interest remain fixed. Most people, however, include insurance and taxes into their monthly mortgage, so if those rates rise, your monthly payments can increase even though you have a fixed-rate mortgage.

Just as with car payments, being able to afford the monthly payments doesn't mean a fixed-rate mortgage is without risk. It's always best to take out mortgages with lower monthly payments than what you think you can afford. Always budget for the possibility that your monthly "fixed rate" payment will increase. If you create your financial plans based on the maximum you can afford each month, you'll have no room for errors, and that means it's only a matter of time before Murphy's Law prevails. That is, if anything can go wrong, it will. Personal finances are filled with uncertainties. Jobs are lost, food and gas prices rise, stock markets crash, and unexpectedly large expenses happen. The day you buy new car tires, your water heater will begin leaking and then your roof.

If you own your own business and live the life of an entrepreneur, like me, you may be intimately familiar with Murphy's Law. Keep enough cash on hand to allow for the unknowns that are bound to occur. Most financial planners suggest keeping at least six months' worth of living expenses on hand. Keeping monthly payments low—and extra cash on hand—is a great plan for reducing risk.

One of the best ways to get fantastic borrowing rates and keep monthly payments low is to have a great credit score. It's one of the most misunderstood and overlooked aspects of financial planning.

Credit Scores

For any economy to expand, it helps to allow those who have idle cash on hand to lend it to those who can put it to use. Banks, for example, sit on large piles of cash from depositors, who'd like to earn some type of return on that money. This is usually done by lending it to others to buy cars, boats, and homes, or to pay off credit cards, student loans, or other expenses.

But how can a lender tell if someone is trustworthy and will be able to repay their debts? That's where credit scores come in. A credit score is a way of assessing people's creditworthiness by looking at various factors on their credit reports.

Just about anything you do that requires credit will make its way to your credit report. If you're making mortgage payments, car payments, or using credit cards, they'll get reported. Even though you need credit to get utilities or power turned on, they aren't usually reported. However, some will report to credit bureaus upon request. If you have a good history with these departments but have no other history, you may inquire if they'll report your payments to the credit bureaus. Anything helps.

Credit reports show various information, such as the number of open accounts, type of account (credit card, car loan, home mortgage), date account opened, credit limit, and any negative remarks (such as liens or unpaid debts). Several companies provide credit ratings services, and their algorithms calculate a credit score based on information in your credit report. The idea is to create a scoring system that helps to predict a person's creditworthiness.

Each company claims to have a better scoring model than the next, but there's only so many ways you can slice and dice the relatively small amount of information on a credit report. Most of the time, your score from one company will be fairly close to that of another. Under most models, the two biggest factors are the percentage of on-time payments (35%) and credit utilization ratio (30%). Those two factors account for 65% of your score.

The credit utilization ratio shows how much of your credit you're using. If you have one credit card with a $5,000 limit but have a $1,000 balance, your credit utilization ratio is 20%. Most of the credit reporting agencies like to see that you're using 30% or less of your credit limit. Your score will begin to drop sharply if you exceed that amount.

Credit companies also consider the average age of credit, total number of accounts, and total number of credit inquiries. History longer than nine years is considered excellent, but five years is usually sufficient to get great credit scores and lower-interest-rate loans. You can't rush time. If you're applying for a home loan, you can't get five years' worth of history by next month. That's why it's best to begin building credit sooner rather than later.

Probably the most widely used credit rating agency is Fair Isaac and Company, more commonly known as FICO. Established by Bill Fair and Earl Isaac in 1956, FICO is considered to be the gold standard of rating agencies. Many major lenders will rely solely on your FICO score to make decisions. With FICO, your credit score will range between 300 and 850. Each lender makes its decisions on what's an acceptable score, but a score around 620 or higher is probably adequate to receive a credit card or home loan.

However, FICO is not the only game in town. There's competition. TransUnion, Equifax, and Experian are three other major reporting agencies that offer different scoring models. In 2006, these three companies entered into a joint venture and created a scoring model called VantageScore, which used a scale ranging from 501 to 900. In 2013, they updated the model to VantageScore 3.0, which now uses the same 300 to 850 scale as FICO to make easier comparisons. If you've earned a high credit score, you're deemed to be a good credit risk, which means you have a high probability of paying back your loans.

Credit scores have an important economic function because they allow lenders to quickly assess the risk of any loan without knowing much about the person applying. Without credit scores, lenders would have to take people through lengthy applications. Even then, they'd never have as much confidence in their decisions since long credit histories tell better stories of how people have used—or abused—credit.

The main thing to understand is that each agency calculates risk factors in different ways, and your credit score from one company may be quite different from that of another. Further, each lender may create their own scoring model or make adjustments to existing scoring models, so there are technically hundreds of scoring models. But if your score is relatively high under one model, it should be reasonably close under the standards of other models.

Sooner Is Better

Credit scores will play a big part in your financial future, and that means you should start early to develop a credit history. About 15% of your credit score comes from the length of time you've had credit. Unfortunately, many people believe it's best to avoid credit altogether. Who wants to owe anybody anything?! As we've already discussed, when you're paying interest to someone, that's money you're not earning in another investment.

Well, even if you never plan to use credit, in today's society you need to have good credit history for nearly everything. If you want to rent an apartment—credit check. You want the lights turned on? Credit check. Cable installed? Credit check. How about a phone, security system, or car insurance? Yep, credit checks.

Credit, however, goes beyond just getting your home up and running. Today, many businesses require a credit check before they'll employ you, especially if you'll have access to cash, such as a banker or cashier would. Bad credit scores are the result of high debts or defaulted debts, which means there's potentially a high temptation to steal. Whether it's a valid assumption or not, many employers now assume that a bad credit score equals a high-risk employee. Who'd think your entire career could be on the line from a bad credit score?

Develop a credit history early, but also start small. Just because you get a credit card doesn't mean you need to go out and charge an exotic Hawaiian vacation. If you use a credit card just to pay your cell phone bill each month, for instance, it counts.

Always be sure to keep extra cash on hand to plan for unexpected expenses. Otherwise, you'll end up pulling out the plastic to meet those needs—and that may be the beginning of the end. Credit card companies don't give you a special break just because you lost your job. Keeping cash on hand is part of the art of managing debt. If your balances reach a point where you can just make the minimum payments, it can be nearly impossible to escape the debt trap, and high balances and missed payments will stay on your report for years.

Starting early has another big benefit. As stated previously, about 15% of your credit score comes from the average length of time your credit has been opened. One of the problems with using the average time is that it can be greatly reduced by the addition of a single card. If you have one card that's been open for 10 years, but you open another one today, your average history is cut in half. That could significantly drop your score.

Chances are, as your career advances, you'll need other cards. Perhaps ones that provide frequent-flyer miles, offer lower interest rates, or give better perks. If you have several cards that have long histories, the addition of a single card isn't going to make a significant difference to your average. But if you open several cards over a short time, your average length of time can be reduced to dangerously low levels. But with a lengthy credit history, you can avoid these problems, so start early.

The Credit Dilemma

Establishing credit is critical for today's society, but it's also a double-edged sword. Having access to credit lowers buying resistance. That means you're more likely to buy things you don't really need. Economics shows that when prices are lower, people have the incentive to buy more. Credit gives the illusion that things are cheaper and easier to come by. You may not have the cash today, but you can still take it home if you have a credit card. Problems appear to be solved.

That's why stores prefer that you use your credit card rather than cash—you're likely to buy more stuff. So, on the one hand, it seems you're better off to avoid the use of credit. However, having a great credit score means you'll get better mortgage rates and have lower monthly payments. With lower payments, you'll have more money to invest, pay for college, and use for other opportunities.

There's always a tradeoff, and if you're spending more on mortgages because of bad credit, it sets off a dangerous round of financial repercussions. To get a good mortgage interest rate, you'll need to have a good credit score. It's impossible to get one—or boost it significantly—in a short time, so it's best to begin early. As we've already learned, most credit history is created from credit cards, but any type of credit will count, be it personal credit lines, store cards, auto loans, or any other type that reports to credit bureaus.

Without a credit score, you can probably forget about a home loan unless you have a bunch of money to plunk down. This is where you enter into the credit score dilemma: you need to establish credit, but to do so, you must use credit—and it doesn't come cheap. Credit cards can now charge rates upwards of 30% per year. Unless you can pay off a big chunk of that balance each month, you'll never get out from under the debt. A $5,000 balance at 18% can take longer than 20 years to pay off if you just pay the monthly minimums. And the amount of interest you'll pay may be more than triple the amount you borrowed.

Of course, when you apply for a card, you'll have the best intentions of never letting your balances get out of control. That's what everyone thinks, and it's exactly why credit card companies are eager to get that card in your hands. Once you have a credit card, it's only a matter of time before other necessary major expenses occur—new tires, water heater, or doctors' visits, for instance—and that's what keeps the debt piling on and prevents you from getting out from underneath it.

Just as when figuring out how much to borrow for a home loan, always keep credit card balances at levels where you can afford to pay a significant portion each month, say at least 20%. The temptation is that the minimum monthly required payment will be low, maybe only $10, but continuously pay just the minimum and you'll be in debt for eternity.

What about the other extreme? Is it a good idea to pay off the balance in full each month? Many people believe that paying off your balance in full has a negative impact on your score. That's not really true. If you're using credit cards continually, or at least quite often, you'll always have a balance from month to month. Each month, there's a cutoff date, and a snapshot of the amount due is taken at that time. But there will likely be charges made after that cutoff date that aren't reflected. Instead, they'll show up on next month's bill. The point is that if you pay off your balance each month, the credit agencies see you're managing debt over time. That's what's most important.

It's a myth that you need to rack up large balances and pay hefty interest charges over time to get a good credit score. At the same time, what you don't want to do is get a credit card and then never use it. The possession of a credit card isn't what establishes credit; it's the managed use of debt over time. In fact, if you let a card sit idle too long, the issuer may cancel the card, which could damage your credit score because it could increase your utilization ratio and also decrease your average age of credit.

If you're serious about establishing good credit, get a credit or charge card and use it to pay a few monthly bills, such as your cable or cell phone. And don't forget that the likes of Uber and Amazon don't take cash. You don't have to charge a lot, but you do need a long history. Credit can be a double-edged sword, but the lack of credit usually cuts far worse.

Credit Cards or Charge Cards?

When researching the right credit card for you, you may hear about charge cards. The most common is a "traditional" American Express card. These are different from credit cards (Visa, MasterCard, and Discover, plus some forms of American Express).

In many ways, charge cards are the same as credit cards and are usually accepted at the same places. With charge cards, however, you're required to pay off the entire balance each month. It's not a revolving line of credit that you can pay off over time, as you can with a credit card. A charge card can be a benefit since it reduces the temptation to build up big debts. By requiring bills to be paid in full each month, borrowers monitor themselves and make sure they're not spending more than they can afford.

However, while charge cards can keep you from building up big debts, they can also back you into a corner if money is unexpectedly tight one month. Remember Murphy? If you don't pay off your charge card in full each month, the penalties charged greatly outweigh the interest charges from credit cards. It'll also damage your credit score.

Some people believe that charge cards don't allow you to build credit in the same way as a credit card. Not true. As discussed in the previous section, even when you pay off the monthly amount, there will likely be new charges unaccounted for, which means you're effectively managing debt over time. Whether you use a credit card or charge card, the important point is to use it to build credit.

Charge cards sometimes seem attractive because they advertise that there are no interest charges since you pay the balance in full each month. However, these cards also carry high annual fees—ranging from $95 to $450—depending on the perks they offer. These high annual fees amount to nothing more than an upfront interest charge. For example, if you carry an average balance of $2,500 on a credit card for an entire year, you'd pay $450 in interest charges if rates are 18%. Whether the company charges you 18% per year or $450 up front, it should make no difference to you. They're basically the same thing. So a downside to high annual fees is that you must use the card often and charge a lot to make them worthwhile. But if you find a charge card that offers great perks, by all means get one.

If the idea of a charge card isn't appealing, you can create the same "no interest" benefit with credit cards. Most credit cards offer a grace period, which is about 21 days between the end of a billing cycle and the date your payment is due. If you pay your balance in full during the grace period, you'll incur no interest charges.

If you're diligent about keeping balances low and paying them off at the end of each month, a credit card can act as a charge card—but without the high annual fees. Using credit cards in this way also has a benefit since you're not required to pay the entire balance. If money's unexpectedly tight, at least you have the opportunity to make a smaller payment without negatively affecting your credit score.

Still, the lure of making small monthly payments by carrying a balance is exactly what causes so many people to get trapped in unmanageable credit card debt. Again, be sure to keep balances at manageable levels. If you're good about keeping balances low, you're probably better off with a credit card in the event you can't pay off the entire balance at the end of the month. That relief can go a long way to maintaining a high credit score.

That said, charge cards can still shine because of rewards that accompany them. Most assign a point value for each dollar you spend, and you can redeem these points across many categories, ranging from travel to shopping or even statement credits. Charge cards can be a great alternative for debit cards, provided you use them for things you'd normally buy anyway: gas, groceries, cable bills, and other monthly expenses. The rewards can actually put money in your pocket and easily justify the annual fees. As a side note, if the card you carry (charge or credit) offers any reward system, always opt for the cash-back option rather than the "points" option if you have the choice.

A charge card will add to your credit history. Your debit card won't. Debit cards create another potential problem. Under the federal Electronic Fund Transfer Act, you're not liable for any loss or theft on your card—provided you immediately report the card lost or stolen and that it hasn't been used. In other words, as long as the bank hasn't incurred any losses, neither will you. Thanks!

However, if you report the problems within two business days after realizing the card is missing or hacked, you're accountable for the first $50 in losses. After that, you could be liable for $500—or an unlimited amount if you don't notify the bank within 60 days after your statement is mailed to you. With credit or charge cards, you're legally held to the first $50 in losses once you report the missing or hacked card (although most won't even make you pay that). You're not liable for any charges after you report the card. If your bank information is hacked and people are making fraudulent charges, a credit card or charge card can be a lifesaver when compared to a debit card.

So, once again, for those who wish to pay for everything with cash and never use credit, the economics of credit and charge cards make them worth your attention. If you're looking for a charge card, American Express now has a monopoly on the market. Diners Club used to issue charge cards, but they've stopped accepting applications. American Express, however, will likely require a good established credit score—probably 680 or higher—before you'll get accepted.

Whether you choose a credit card or charge card doesn't matter much to your credit history, provided you're keeping timely payments. Most companies allow you to set up an automatic minimum payment through their websites. It's a great idea to set up auto payments in the event you happen to forget. A missed payment stays on your credit report for two years.

If you're just starting out and trying to build credit, you're probably better off using credit cards, such as Visa, MasterCard, or Discover, so that you have an escape hatch, just in case your money runs a bit short at the end of the month. Just be sure you're disciplined enough not to rack up unmanageable debts. The temptation to buy now and pay later can be irresistible. It's exactly what makes the credit card industry thrive—and causes people to make bad financial decisions.

Big-Ticket Items

Economists like to classify various types of goods. There are normal goods, inferior goods, Giffen goods, and the list goes on. *Big-ticket items* are those with relatively high price tags, such as houses, cars, boats, home theaters, and major appliances. Usually these goods also fall under another category called *durable goods* because they create benefits for the owner for extended periods of time, usually defined as three years or more.

We have already touched on it a bit, but I personally prefer to buy used cars. I've also found that I can save big buying many durable goods secondhand. Craigslist, eBay, Amazon, garage sales, and auctions are all places where you can save hundreds, even thousands, on your big-ticket items.

But not everyone wants to buy a used washing machine or lawnmower on Craigslist, so here are some tips for when you want to buy new or finance a purchase. Because of the relatively high costs, people often buy big-ticket items on credit, so these goods are interest-rate sensitive. Consumer purchases will vary inversely with interest rates. That is, as interest rates fall, the quantity demanded increases. When interest rates rise, the quantity demanded falls.

It's easy to see the connection once you realize that higher interest rates increase your total cost. When interest rates are low, as they are now (they may be slowly rising, but they're still historically low as of this writing), you're more likely to buy a car since the overall cost will be reduced. It's the Law of Demand in disguise: people buy more when prices are low; however, when interest rates are high, you're less likely to buy a car since the total cost will be far greater.

The connection is more difficult to see for those who don't use credit. But if interest rates are high, people are less likely to buy big-ticket items—even if they use cash. For example, if you can afford to buy a car outright with cash, you're still less likely to do it if interest rates are high. That's because there's a large opportunity cost, and you could earn more interest by keeping your cash. The money used to buy the car can no longer be used to earn interest.

Let's say you finance a $20,000 car, but pay an additional $3,000 interest; it's no different than paying $20,000 cash and missing out on $3,000 worth of interest that you could have made by investing that money. Both scenarios netted $23,000 in total cost. If you don't like paying $3,000 in interest, you also wouldn't like missing out on $3,000 in interest income.

Just as time always creates an opportunity cost for people, interest creates opportunity cost for money. People can't be in two different places at once, and money can't be spent twice. That's why interest rates should always play a big role in your decisions when buying big-ticket items, whether with cash or card.

When car shopping, everything is negotiable, including the interest rate. It may not sound like much, but shaving off one percentage point (from 5% to 4%, for example) can make a big difference over the life of a loan. If you buy a $25,000 car and finance it for 60 months, you'll save more than $600 by reducing your interest rate by just one percentage point.

As you learned at the beginning of the chapter, the tactic a car salesman uses is to find out how much a potential buyer can afford to pay monthly. If you say $350, for example, the salesman knows your "magic number." If he could have swung the deal for $320, there's no reason now for him to do so. Also, by setting a monthly payment, the salesman can easily put you in a more expensive car with a longer-term loan to get the payments where you want them. But without understanding the financial side and the role of interest rates, you'll likely end up with a bad deal—and paying on the car longer.

Always negotiate the interest rate first. Better yet, go to a bank or credit union and get pre-approved for a car loan before you go car shopping. Do your financial negotiations off the dealer's lot and you'll make better financial decisions on it. That way you're not too anxious when staring at the car you really want. You'll be less likely to let your emotions take over, saying yes to any deal that can meet your monthly payment.

Another dilemma new car buyers face is the "cash versus interest rate" offers used by dealers. Car manufacturers often run promotions where you can choose between an upfront cash offer, say $1,000, or a low interest rate, say 2%. In almost all cases, the interest rate is the better deal, yet most buyers immediately jump on the cash. Many websites provide calculators that show the savings you make by accepting one deal over the other. Be sure to check the numbers.

Aside from the financial aspects, economics can also shed light on the optimal times to buy big-ticket goods. If you're car shopping, it's best to do it when the new models are introduced. As the supply of new cars hits the dealers' lots, the average price of cars comes down. It's best to hold out until the supply of cars is high and dealers have the incentive to move inventory.

Another tactic is to look in the showroom for the person who has won "salesperson of the month" most often in recent months. You'll usually see photos of recent winners displayed somewhere highly visible. *That's* the person likely to move the most cars, so you'll want to deal with her.

Go to the dealership a few times and get the salesperson to invest lots of time in you. That way she'll have a better incentive to move the car; otherwise, she'll see it as wasted time. If you just visit the dealership once for a few minutes without buying anything, the salesperson barely remembers it. But once time is invested, it's a different story. There's a great incentive to make the sale.

Next, wait until near the end of the month. Better yet, wait until the end of a quarter. Most dealers pay generous bonuses to the leading salesperson, and one more car out the door may make the difference between collecting that extra cash or not. In fact, it's possible the salesperson might even sell the car at a slight loss if it greatly increases the chance of a big bonus. Car dealers use guerrilla marketing tactics to hook buyers, make them pay for added features, and accept higher interest rates. There's no reason you can't use economics to keep your money in your pocket.

Remember: all decisions are ultimately financial ones. Every decision impacts your finances—and your future. The best financial deals go to those who understand the economics of decisions and how people respond to incentives.

CHAPTER 11

MAIN STREET TO WALL STREET

You'll probably follow many career paths, but no matter which you choose, one thing will always follow you: Wall Street. Even if you don't plan to actively invest in "the markets," or speculate on the ebb and flow of prices, or get addicted to watching the day-to-day drama, you'll still always have ties to Wall Street. For example, you may participate in company 401(k) plans, invest for your children's education, or try to predict the direction of interest rates to help you determine the best time to buy a home. Like it or not, it pays to understand the economics of Wall Street.

What Is Wall Street?

Wall Street is a physical location, about eight blocks long, in the Financial District of New York City. It's the home of the New York Stock Exchange (NYSE), one of the largest stock exchanges, as well as many of the world's elite brokerage firms and financial businesses.

However, when you hear the term "Wall Street" used in the financial press, it's often used to talk about the US financial markets in general. When people talk about the financial markets, they're talking primarily about stocks and bonds. But there are other dimensions, such as futures, options, swap agreements, and other derivative instruments. Why do we need so many financial instruments?

Well, Wall Street—aka the financial markets—was created to allow for a more efficient formation of capital. In any society, you have people with great ideas, but they need money to make them come true. Those great ideas may become large corporations, providing much-needed goods and services and creating hundreds of thousands of jobs. In that same society, you'll also have people who may not have ideas but who do have money sitting idle in a savings account. Wouldn't it be great if those with extra money could loan it to those with great ideas and get a nice return on their investment?

The financial markets, through the many different instruments, allow for those with savings to quickly channel it to those with attractive investment ideas. It's not just the person with the great ideas or those who lend the money who win. The consumer wins as well. Without financial markets, we wouldn't have cars, televisions, cell phones, and all the other wonderful, life-changing technologies we enjoy. Or at least these advances wouldn't have appeared so quickly.

The faster new products reach the market, the quicker new technology can be developed. The entire nation and world become better off as the economy grows at a much faster pace than otherwise would have occurred. Everybody wins when you can efficiently connect buyers and sellers.

Taking a Company Public

If you have a great moneymaking idea, how can it become a reality? Without financial markets, you'd have to find investors and sell them your idea. I told you about my bedsheet company, My Side and Yours, back in chapter 2. As a small start-up company, this is exactly what I had to do, and as you learned, it didn't work too well for me.

But even if you find investors, do you think anyone's going to say, "Here's the check. Please remember me when you make millions from your great idea"? It's never happened to me, and it probably never will. Developing business ideas in this way could take years. It would be extremely hard to raise money to get your idea off the ground. The long process and resulting frustrations mean that most great ideas would never make it past the drawing board.

With My Side and Yours, it took almost a full year to bring the product to market, but that wasn't the challenge. The challenge was funding the costs of launching the company and shouldering the loss until we could become profitable through sales. But that's not necessary with a financial market; the process becomes relatively easy(er) and fast(er).

It begins by forming a corporation. Anyone can create one for just a few hundred bucks. One person can create it, or an entire group can do so. Regardless of how many people start the corporation, in the eyes of the law, it's viewed as an individual person. And that means a corporation can be taxed, it can be sued, and it can be publicly traded.

What does it mean to be publicly traded? With a corporation, shares of stock are created, which are nothing more than fictitious pieces of paper. The number is purely arbitrary, but, for example, a corporation may begin with 10 million shares. Regardless of the number of shares, they're allowed to be sold to investors.

If a company has 10 million shares outstanding and you buy one million shares, you'd own 10% of the company and would be entitled to 10% of the profits. By creating shares of stock, the corporation can easily be divided up among many owners, and it becomes easy(er) to transfer ownership. If someone doesn't want to own his share of the company anymore, it's easy to transfer that ownership to another investor by selling the shares.

If you create a company with a great story of potential success, large underwriters, such as Goldman Sachs or JP Morgan, may be willing to sell those shares, primarily to its clients, in exchange for hefty fees. Let's say Goldman Sachs decides to underwrite your company. It may cut a $50 million check in exchange for your 10 million shares. In return, it has its brokers contact all of its clients to pitch your story to them. Goldman may have paid $5 per share for your company, but they may turn around and sell them for $20 per share to public investors.

When shares are sold in this way, it's called an initial public offering, or IPO. It's also called the *primary market*. After the IPO, the once privately held company becomes a publicly traded corporation. It's no longer owned by a single person but instead by thousands or millions of investors.

By selling shares through the IPO, the original owner loses a lot of control over the business, must publicly disclose earnings, and falls under close investor and government scrutiny. However, the big advantage is the ease with which cash is generated to put ideas to work. Despite the loss of some control, most founders will retain majority voting rights and therefore still retain control of the company's vision.

If you buy shares of stock during an IPO, how will you ever sell those shares in the future? That's where the stock market comes in. The stock market serves as a *secondary market* where shares can be freely bought and sold among investors. Think of it like a used-car market. When General Motors (GM) sells a Corvette to a dealer, that's like the IPO market. That's the only time GM receives money from the sale. However, if you buy the car from a dealer and then sell it at a later date, that's the used-car market.

A good friend of mine has owned a 1966 Corvette since 1971 and recently met the man who originally owned the car. Owners can freely sell a car numerous times—even back to a previous owner—but each sale takes place in the used market. General Motors never sees a dime from any sale in the used market. Of course, GM may choose to raise more money by selling more shares, which is called a *secondary offering*. It's only in this sense that the company would benefit from rising share prices.

The stock market is just a formal used market. If you buy shares of stock after an IPO, you're buying "used" shares. They're shares that were already in existence. Like that 1966 Corvette, shares of stock can be worth more than they were originally. Just because that 1966 Corvette is worth more now, GM does not make any extra money if my friend were to sell his Corvette today. When shares of stock are traded in the stock market, the company never sees any of that money. The only money received was from the IPO or secondary offering. So if you hear that the price of International Business Machines (IBM) shares went up today, that cash is not going to IBM. It just means the price of shares in the stock market—the used market—is increasing.

Most large companies you're used to hearing about are publicly traded. Each company is identified with a code, usually one to four letters, called a ticker symbol. For example, Apple's ticker is AAPL, Coca-Cola's is KO, Amazon's is AMZN, McDonald's is MCD, and Walmart's is WMT. If you ever want to know the current price of any publicly traded company, you simply type the ticker into any number of free websites and find the current stock price. Even a Google search will do.

Unlike most other prices in the world, share prices can rise and fall rapidly. If everyone suddenly decides to buy stock in a company because of positive upcoming news, share prices can rise dramatically. And of course if news is bad, prices can fall with equal furor. So the value of any company can quickly change, and that's one of the reasons so many are fascinated by the stock market; it can almost become a casino-style game.

When prices change quickly, it's often difficult to know exactly why. All we know for sure is that the changing price reflects the market's current opinion. It's the result of all investors' "buy" and "sell" orders. While uncommon, the value of a company can change by 20%—or far more—in a single day. Most of the time, prices change by a small percentage up or down every second of every day.

If the majority of stock prices fall substantially, it's called a market crash. While there's no formal definition of a crash, they're usually characterized by a rapid decline in prices, say 10% or so, over a period of days. Crashes are mostly due to crowd psychology and positive feedback loops. That is, once prices begin to fall, more investors get nervous and sell, which pushes prices lower, which makes even more investors sell, which pushes prices lower yet, and on goes the process.

Each price drop encourages a new group of investors to sell. Most crashes are therefore a self-fulfilling prophecy. If everybody thinks market prices will continue to lower, they will. Extreme market crashes, like the Crash of '87, can happen quickly, furiously, and without any apparent reason. It's the equivalent of getting dumped by the market!

Now see if you can use economics to answer a common question new investors often ask: is it possible for any company to run out of shares in the market? In other words, if everyone decides to buy, isn't it possible that the exchanges would run out of shares to sell? The answer is no, and the reason is price. The Law of

Supply says that as share prices rise, it entices sellers, which releases shares back into the market. At the same time, the Law of Demand says that people will buy fewer shares when the price is higher. So higher prices means more sellers—and fewer buyers—enter the market.

The reverse is true when markets fall. As prices get lower, more buyers and fewer sellers appear. Eventually, price must equalize. That's why, after a crash, you'll see a new base price begin to form, called the floor. Once the price gets low enough, many buyers will appear and stop prices from falling further. Just as price guarantees we'll never run out of oil, it also ensures we'll never run out of shares.

Three Major Functions

The stock market serves three major functions, and there is some overlap among them. First, a stock market provides an allocation function. By now you should realize that's done by a pricing system. By allowing buyers and sellers to meet at one central location, it's easy to calculate a price that equalizes each party.

For example, at any moment of the day, if there are thousands of buyers and only half as many sellers, the price must rise. As the price rises, some buyers back out while new sellers appear. As the price adjusts, eventually you'll end up with an equal number of buyers and sellers. A stock market makes it incredibly easy to figure out how many shares of stock are needed at any moment to balance supply and demand.

Second, a stock market creates information transparency. The best way to determine the shares' value is to have a single system where all buyers' and sellers' prices can be recorded. The stock market gives us the average value of what investors think shares are worth. Without a stock market to reflect public opinion, it would be impossible to truly say what shares are worth.

What's a company worth? Without a stock market, it would be difficult to say. Would you rather trust the opinion of a few certified public accountants or the collective opinion of the world? When everyone is watching and evaluating, you're going to get a really good estimate of what a business is actually worth.

The value of any publicly traded company can be found by taking the number of shares in the secondary market and multiplying that by the current market price, which is called the *market capitalization*, or market cap for short. For example, in mid-2016 there were 5.5 billion shares of Apple (AAPL) trading in the secondary market at a price of nearly $100 per share. So the value of Apple, as viewed by the market, was about $550 billion.

On the other hand, shares of Chipotle Mexican Grill (CMG) were trading for about $400 per share, with 29.2 million shares in the market. The value of CMG was therefore about $11.6 billion. Even though Chipotle's $400 single share market price is greater than Apple's $100 single share market price, it doesn't mean Chipotle is worth more as a business. Apple was simply divided into more pieces (shares) so that the price per share was lower. Apple's share price is lower, but Apple's market cap is nearly 50 times greater.

As new information hits the market, investors react. If it's good news, prices rise; if the news is bad, prices fall. While no single person can know every bit of news floating around in the world that might affect a certain stock, the market somehow knows. Because every buy and sell order is executed through one exchange, all information is assimilated into prices—that's transparency. Without that information, sellers would be reluctant to sell and buyers reluctant to buy. The ability for businesses to raise capital quickly would disappear.

The third big benefit of a stock market is that it provides confidence for investors to buy and sell shares. You're much more likely to buy shares if you know you can sell them in a matter of seconds if you want to get out. Without a stock market, you'd have to locate a buyer on your own. That could take months and be expensive.

One of the main areas I specialize in, with the consulting company I own, is doing exactly that: helping people buy, sell, and finance companies. It typically takes three to six months for most small (under $5 million) transactions to be finalized, but I have worked on deals that literally take years to complete.

With a stock market, however, just click a button and your shares are instantly sold at the current market price. It's also just as easy to buy. If you hear information that makes you believe a particular company will do well in the future, you can quickly purchase shares—and capitalize on your outlook if you're correct. Because of the speed at which investors can buy and sell shares, all information is instantly revealed in prices.

What's the Fascination with the Market?

We have the *Wall Street Journal*, CNBC, Yahoo! Finance, and Bloomberg, just to name a few. We have brokerage firms, software programs, and an infinite number of books, websites, and videos that give market advice. They're all products of capitalism because we have something else: millions of people trying to predict the direction of market prices.

We probably have more tools and information surrounding the financial markets than any other profession. So what's the fascination? The fascination is that there's no other mechanism like the stock market. In no other market are all purchase and sale prices funneled into one point to reflect the collective opinions of the world.

Check out gas prices around your city and you'll see quite different numbers, even though it's virtually the same product. That's because you have different buyers and sellers acting in their own markets, and you can get different equilibrium prices. You won't find that in the stock market. The price of IBM shares is the same no matter where you buy it.

Because the collective opinion is funneled into one market, there are few ways that offer the lure of making money like the stock market. Sure, some people may make lots of money quickly by gambling, but that's mostly luck. The stock market is different.

We have news, TV, the Internet, books, papers, and magazines all designed to give you a leg up on trading. There's information about past, current, and future earnings. It seems so much easier to guess the direction when you know where everyone thinks prices are going. If you felt that shares of Apple were going to rise, you could buy them today at one price and sell them in the future for a nice profit.

Do it over and over and you'll amass a fortune. It's easy money—or so it seems. Buying low and selling high produces profits. There's no question on the math. But the economics of the financial markets have a different story to tell. And it's important to understand economics if you're to survive financially.

Going Once, Going Twice

The financial markets are a continuous live auction, very much like a big version of my favorite website, eBay. Because everyone is trying to predict the next price move, all current information gets factored into the market almost instantly.

If a stock is trading for $100 per share, but information comes out suggesting it will be worth $105 tomorrow, the market will quickly push the price to $105 today. In other words, as soon as the information is released, everybody wants to buy—and nobody wants to sell. There's an immediate imbalance of buyers, so the price begins to rise. Buying today at $100 becomes an obviously great deal, but so does buying at $101, $102, or any price less than $105. However, if the price hits $105 today, there's no reason to push it any higher, so people stop bidding and the price stabilizes at $105.

In the stock market, the biggest rewards go to those who buy first upon hearing news. Because the entire world is watching, as soon as news is released—or is believed to be released—share prices rise immediately, which gives us one of the most quoted pieces of trading advice: "Buy the rumor, and sell the news."

The problem with trying to make fast money in the market is that everybody is trying to do the same thing. If you buy the stock today just because you think the price will rise in the future, chances are, the gain you want was already built into the price. In the stock market business, we say the market is "forward looking," which means the market doesn't care what happened yesterday. That's the past, and the market already knows about that. The market instead is always trying to figure out what prices will be in the future.

The fact that every trader is trying to accomplish the same thing should be a big hint that making sure-fire profits can't be easy. You can't beat the market by using the same information as everyone else. If everyone has access to the same information, there's no way that an individual trader can gain a long-run advantage.

Think of the market as similar to being stuck in rush-hour traffic. All drivers are trying to accomplish the same thing: to get home as quickly as possible. In doing so, drivers seek out any information that will provide an edge—watching for the fastest lanes, spotting a stalled car up ahead, and looking for merging lanes. If one driver thinks he can gain an advantage by switching lanes, that new lane slows down a bit since there's now an additional car. The lane he left, however, speeds up a bit since there's now one less car. So, if all drivers are doing the same thing, the faster lanes will slow down while the slower ones will speed up, until there's no incentive to switch lanes. At that point, all lanes are moving at the same speed, and you're stuck in traffic.

If you understand how lanes equalize in rush-hour traffic, you should be able to see that the same process occurs in the stock market. This is the idea of the *efficient-market hypothesis*, which simply states that it's impossible to consistently find profitable opportunities because everyone is trying to do the same thing.

You shouldn't expect to beat the overall market averages by doing what everyone else is doing. You shouldn't expect to be correct in the majority of cases any more than you should expect to always predict the fastest lane. The second you think you see a faster lane and switch to it, there's a chance there'll be an unforeseen accident ahead and you'll actually end up worse off.

All investors are trying to do the same thing: find profits. If there's any information that suggests the price will rise (a faster lane), traders respond to that incentive by purchasing the shares (switching lanes). Doing so, however, raises the price of those shares a bit and reduces the potential profit. The bigger the potential for profits, the more buyers will decide to buy that stock and the faster the price rises.

Information travels nearly instantly in the stock market. By the time you see any news that suggests there's easy money, remember you're driving in rush-hour traffic. Everyone sees that news, and it quickly gets factored into the price. Buying the shares—just like changing lanes—probably isn't going to make a significant difference. This is why it's so difficult to make the "easy" money so many trading websites and books profess is possible. If it was as easy as they say, they'd be keeping it secret—not trying to sell these magnificent moneymaking skills to you for a few hundred bucks.

Investing versus Trading

When it comes to making money in the market, there are two basic approaches: investing and trading. Investors take long-term views. They act as owners of the company, realizing there will be ups and downs while holding on for the long-term increases in value that inevitably come from a well-run business.

Investing in the market is like a marriage. My wife is a saint. She's put up with me for years and is a wonderful mother to our two boys, but she had no idea what she was getting into when she said "I do" back in 2004. You're in it for the long haul, for better, for worse. It's the same with investing.

If you're patient, you can consistently make money in the long run. If you look at the price charts of most stocks, or any major index, there's a long-term upward bias. Sure, there are bumps along the way, but in the long run you'll see that prices tend to rise. Investors are looking for that long-term increase and are willing to ride out the short-term bumps.

Some people, however, don't have the patience for the long run. They prefer to trade in and out of stocks quickly. They buy right before they think a stock's price will rise and sell at the first sign of profits. They're in, they're out. Trading, for them, is like dating. There's no commitment and nothing long term about it. It's pure speculation, hoping for big gains in a short time.

Trading can be fun and provide the adrenaline rush that traders live for. There's nothing quite like buying shares just before a highly anticipated earning's report with the plan to sell as soon as the share price jumps.

As someone who used move commodities on a trading floor for a living and still dabbles in the market, I can tell you I've never been wrong on a trade. But, man, has my timing been off! I've even given my own family and friends bad advice when I felt confident that the market was due for a big correction. Timing is everything, and the very thought of a missed rally can be as frustrating as a big loss.

I have lived it; I know firsthand what those losses feel like, and there's a big danger for those who don't understand the economics of how financial markets work. Remember, everyone is trying to do the same thing. The problem with trading is that you'll end up spending tons of money in commissions but find there's very little profit in it for you.

Stock traders also feel they reduce the risk of losses by quickly buying and selling. They think if they can buy just before prices rise and then sell for a quick profit, they'll avoid any large losses. Their philosophy is that they'll make lots of small gains and greatly limit losses. But just like drivers who feel they'll always benefit from changing lanes, they quickly find that they can't always guess the direction of the market.

Trading has a more sinister side. People are risk averse, which means they despise losses. They'll do everything they can to avoid losses. So when traders get caught in a downturn, their reaction is to hang on and try to gamble their way out. The result is that they eventually end up taking a handful of very large losses, which greatly overshadow the small gains.

Even though you'll always hear about "successful traders" and how some website offers a new breed of trading and information, in reality their success (if it exists at all) is short-lived and likely only comes from the monthly fees they collect from others. If you want to make real money in the market, you have to understand investing and the long-term effects of compounding.

The Magic of Compounding

On average, the overall market returns about 7% to 10% per year. In other words, prices rise about that much each year. It's not a ton, but it beats inflation. However, it's not the relatively small increases each year that make investing worthwhile. It's the magic of compounding.

Compounding is the effect of earning interest on interest, which is mathematically like earning money for nothing. Like risk, though, it's a double-edged sword. When applied to debt, it's the force that can keep you in credit card debt forever. When used for investing, it can make you wealthy over time.

If you earn 10% per year, you'd think you'd earn 20% in two years. However, if you invest $100 and earn 10%, you'll have $110 at the end of the first year. You earned $10. If you earn another 10% the following year, you'll earn more because your balance is more. After two years, you'd have $121. An extra dollar appeared out of nowhere. It's the result of interest on interest—money for nothing.

Okay, one dollar may not be much to get worked up about. But the real power of compounding comes from the long-term effects. Eventually, the money earned on the interest will be greater than the amount earned on your initial investment. For instance, $100 earning 10% for 20 years will grow to $673. If there was no compounding effect, that 10% earned on $100 is a flat $10 per year, giving you just $200 after 20 years. That's $473 less than what compounding gives you for doing nothing.

Compounding provides the biggest benefit of long-term investing. Sure, there'll be some bad years, but there'll also be great ones to balance them out. Again, overall, the stock market has a long-term upward bias in prices, so you'll make money in the long run. Time is your most powerful weapon when it comes to investing. Compounding is the reason.

Investing for the Long Haul

Most people find the stock market mysteriously complex and usually end up making bad decisions—or paying for worthless information. But investing can be easy. If you're ever given the opportunity to invest in the stock market, such as with company 401(k) plans, it's best to invest in a broad-based market index, such as the S&P 500.

That index represents 500 of the largest capitalized companies, and it's the hardest index to beat. Each year, the majority of the world's best money managers can't outperform this index. It's an easy choice to make, and it will be the simplest way to make money over the long run. If any one of the companies in the index has a bad year, you've got 499 others to prop it up.

Nearly all 401(k) plans will offer investments in the S&P 500 index. If not, they'll have another broad-based index that will behave similarly. If you decide to make money by trading, don't be surprised if you're met with lackluster results at best and big losses at worst. You'll win some, you'll lose some, but you'll pay commissions with each trade. Each commission and each loss digs the hole a little deeper.

Warren Buffett, CEO of Berkshire Hathaway, is the personification of long-term investing. His favorite holding period is "forever," and he invests as if he were founder and operator of the company. He invests for the long haul. Check his track record and you'll see he's shattered every record in the investing world.

Making money in the financial markets is easy to do over the long run. It all comes down to being patient and holding on through the ups and downs. You'll find many websites promising the road to riches by following their advice.

Remember, however, that people respond to incentives. As long as investors believe that "experts" have the ability to predict the market, these "experts" will respond and provide that information for hefty fees.

But all investors are trying to do the same thing. If you wouldn't trust a person trying to sell you information that promises to get you home more quickly in rush-hour traffic by telling you which lanes to select and when to switch, you shouldn't get too excited about those promising easy money by trading. As Mr. Buffett says, "Wall Street is the only place that people ride to in a Rolls Royce to get advice from those who take the subway." If you decide to trade in and out of the market quickly, you're trying to beat the market by using exactly the same information as everyone else. It's not a recipe for long-term success.

To achieve financial freedom, you have to take some risks. But even more important, you have to approach the markets with marriage in mind and know that you're in it for the long haul. If you decide to play the field, just know that, more likely than not, you'll end up getting continually dumped, and you'll create losses that just may be too big to heal.

CHAPTER 12

WHAT DO INVESTING EXPERTS REALLY KNOW?

Economists are experts in understanding markets, how people respond to incentives, and how supply and demand can alter prices. If you're going to invest in the stock market, it would seem to make sense to turn to an expert for advice.

It's no surprise that many people advertise market-prediction advice and charge high fees for access to their information. They go by different names, ranging from financial experts to professional market timers and, yes, even economists. However, once you understand how the financial markets are organized, you'll see that the information they're giving is far from invaluable. It's more like virtually worthless.

Remember, financial markets are set up so that every single trade is ultimately reported through a single quotation system. The process is a little different between the exchanges (like the NYSE and the NASDAQ), but the ideas are essentially the same.

Because all trades get reported through one system, there can be no differences in price by different dealers. If you want to buy shares of IBM, you'll pay the same price whether you bought from Merrill Lynch or TD Ameritrade. In other words, no broker can claim quality differences in the shares.

In the financial markets, having identical "products" is called *fungible*. That just means one share of IBM is identical to another share of IBM, regardless of where it was purchased. Think of it like money. If you deposit a $100 bill into your checking account, it doesn't matter if you receive that exact $100 bill upon withdrawal. It's all the same. Money is fungible, just like shares of stock. It's the arrangement of having the prices of identical shares filtering through one system that makes the stock market so unique.

Outside of the financial markets, you can find identical products, say a case of Coors Light, but it can have different prices at different stores. You may pay $20 for a case at one store but $25 for an identical case from the convenience store. Or maybe you're Big Enos Burdette, and you're willing to pay the Bandit $80,000 for a truckload of Coors Light. You won't find that happening in the stock market. Everyone gets the identical price because there's only one store: the stock market.

How Prices Change

As we've already discussed, at any time, if you think the market price is too cheap, you can make a profit by purchasing shares and, assuming you're correct, selling when the price rises. If enough people believe prices are too low, you'll have a lot of buyers but few sellers, and that means the price must rise in response.

If a stock is trading for $100, but information makes people believe it will soon be worth $105, profits can be made by all investors who pay less than $105. It's a race to buy, so the price will quickly rise to $105. As news flows throughout the world, any information that's believed to be positive for a stock will get reflected into the price. It's the pursuit of profits that provides the incentive.

On the other hand, if prices are perceived to be too high, a profit can be made by short-selling shares (selling shares you don't own). If enough traders short sell, you'll see more sellers than buyers, and the market price falls in response. The same mechanics that drive prices higher can drive prices lower. Just like buyers, it's the potential for profits that leads traders to short-sell shares if they believe prices are too high.

The only time prices balance is when the market can't quite decipher if the price is too high or too low. There's no reason to buy, and there's no reason to sell. At that moment, the price is considered correct; it's in equilibrium. Even in equilibrium, you'll still see prices change slightly, as there will always be buyers and sellers for a variety of reasons. But to see significant price changes, there needs to be significant news.

Think of the market as a game show where investors can win big cash prizes for correctly voting whether a stock's price is too low, too high, or just right. If prices are believed to be too low, investors "vote" by buying, and if prices are too high, they can "vote" by short-selling shares. As a result, all information gets "baked into" the current price.

Once you understand the architecture of the financial markets, along with the profit incentive, you'll see why it's hard to believe that one "expert" has a better opinion on what a stock's value should be. Information arrives around the world. It's interpreted by different people with different experiences. The collective opinion of the world must be a very good estimate.

That's not to say that the market can't be wrong. It is, often. That's what provides the incentive to invest. However, it doesn't change the fact that the collective opinion includes far more information than one single person could ever offer. While no estimate is perfect, the collective opinion is the best we can ask for.

British Petroleum's Oil Disaster

For instance, when British Petroleum's (BP) oil rig Deepwater Horizon exploded in 2010, 11 workers were killed and nearly five million gallons of oil spilled into the ocean. That's not good news for any company, obviously. But the difficult question is to figure out what the disaster is worth. How far should BP's price fall as a result of the incident?

That depends on what the damage is worth, and the market is the best mechanism to figure it out. Lawyers will have better estimates of potential lawsuits. Accountants will have better estimates of tax and foreign currency exchange consequences. Engineers may have a better idea of what caused the explosion and who's to blame. Oceanographers may have a better understanding of the magnitude of the destruction. And, of course, everyday investors can cast their votes by buying or selling shares based on any number of reasons why they feel the current market price is either too high or too low. But all estimates—good or bad—get factored into the price.

Hold on! If bad estimates get thrown into the mix, doesn't that create a bad estimate? This is where the market's magic happens.

The Market's Magic

While it's true that some investors' estimates will be too low, they'll be counterbalanced by investors with estimates that are equally too high, assuming there are many investors with diverse opinions. On average, they'll hit the mark.

Think of it like throwing darts. If hundreds of people take shots at a dartboard, some throws will be high, but they'll be matched by those that are equally low. Some throws will be far left, but they'll be balanced by those that are far right. With enough participants, each miss will be offset by a miss in the opposite direction. On average, all darts will hit the bullseye.

However, if you ask a world-class dart expert to take *one throw*, he probably won't hit the bullseye. That's just a statistical fact because there's more area outside of the bullseye than inside. This is the same problem you face when you seek expert advice on a stock's value or whether the overall market's valuation is too high or low. You're asking the expert to take one shot.

Instead, if you ask hundreds of people—even amateurs—to take shots and look at the average, this method will outperform the expert's single throw. When you see a stock's current market price, you're looking at the collective opinion of everyone. You're seeing the result of millions of throws at the stock-valuation dartboard.

Going back to the BP disaster, its share price was roughly $60 prior to the explosion. That doesn't mean all investors thought it was worth $60. It's just the collective opinion. It's the price that balances buyers with sellers and is the equivalent to the average price after many throws at the dartboard. For every investor who felt it was worth $55 ($5 lower), there was another who felt it was worth $65 ($5 higher). The two opinions canceled and left both investors hitting the $60 mark, on average.

So, after the explosion, how far should its stock price fall? It was a complex problem with lots of new information hitting the market each day. It all had to be deciphered, and investors cast votes by buying or selling. After two months, BP's share price fell from $60 to $27 (based on the collective opinion of all investors).

Now that you know all of this, does it make sense to approach one "expert" to ask if the $27 price is too high or too low? Any expert can make a bad estimate, but when you have millions of people taking shots, it's hard to believe they all missed the valuation mark. Approach expert advice on whether prices will rise or fall with caution. Just because an expert says a price is too low doesn't mean the market must respond by increasing the price any more than a dart in the hands of an expert is guaranteed to hit the bullseye.

A more dramatic example of the market's magic occurred in 1986, when the space shuttle *Challenger* tragically exploded shortly after takeoff. I was a kid when it happened. I clearly remember being in my grandparents' living room watching the news about it in the days following the explosion. Who was responsible? That was a daunting question, even for NASA engineers. People who ordered parts were not the same as those who assembled the parts, and they were not the same as those who drafted the plans. But somewhere in the long, complex chain, there was an error.

Yet it took the market just 15 minutes to form a good idea of who was at fault. The prices of Lockheed, Martin-Marietta, Morton Thiokol, and Rockwell began falling. They were four key publicly traded companies that had NASA contracts, but only one—Morton Thiokol—fell more than 10%, which caused a trading halt.

A trading halt occurs whenever there's a one-day drop in price that exceeds a certain level, usually 10% for the first halt. During the halt, no trading in that security may take place for typically 15 minutes. It's designed to allow investors a "cooling off" period so that the rapid price changes don't create a psychological sell-off.

Think of the difficulty. Out of the 5,000 or so publicly traded companies, the market knew which companies were possibly going to be affected and which one was the most likely suspect responsible for the explosion—all within minutes. That's what happens when you have millions of people in different fields all seeking profits by interpreting information quickly.

Did the market get it right?

It did!

Two weeks after the accident, after lengthy reviews, Nobel Prize-winning physicist Richard Feynman showed it was Thiokol's faulty 0-rings that caused the booster rockets to fail. What took two weeks for a Nobel Prize winner to find, the market discovered within minutes. That's the difference between asking a single expert and asking millions of people—whether experts or not.

When you throw questions like this to the market, where profits can be made by knowing the answer, someone will know, and the market quickly reveals the answer in the form of prices. Therefore, question the value in seeking out the opinion of one person, no matter how smart or qualified he may appear. He may know a lot, but he can't know it all.

The market's magic can be seen in the old game show *Who Wants to Be a Millionaire?* Contestants were asked a series of multiple choice questions, and if they answered all correctly, they would win a $1 million cash prize. If a contestant wasn't sure of an answer, he could use one of many "lifelines" to get help. One lifeline was called "Phone a Friend," where the contestant could make a single 30-second phone call to one of several pre-determined friends. That's like asking an expert.

However, another lifeline was called "Ask the Audience," where each member of the audience would answer the question by punching in the A, B, C, or D answers on a keypad in front of them. The contestant would see the results in the form of a bar graph, which showed the percentage of the audience that chose each answer.

If you were a contestant and in a dilemma over which lifeline to throw out, which should you choose? Asking a friend produced the right answer about 65% of the time. Not surprisingly, asking the audience had an astounding success rate of 91%. The reason is that any bias is cumulative. If you flip a normal double-sided coin, you only have a 50/50 chance of it coming up heads; there's no way to tell after just one flip. Even if it's a magic trick coin that has a 51% bias, one flip will never prove the bias.

However, that changes when you allow many chances. A biased coin that lands heads 51% of the time will quickly be proven as biased after a couple hundred flips. That small 1% bias will compound. In a similar way, if a contestant chooses to ask the audience, the average person's guess may only be a little better than random. Any individual may be only slightly in favor of one answer, say answer A, which would never show up by asking one person. If you ask hundreds, however, the bias is quickly discovered.

Anyone who has watched the show knows that the bar graph usually had one answer that towered above the remaining three. It was the one most of the audience thought was correct—and it was, 91% of the time. Even though some audience members were fooled, the collective power of the audience revealed the truth.

Seeking Expert Advice

Even though economics tells us that predicting future prices is an educated guess at best, there will always be people who believe some expert can. But if you look at the statistics, you'll see the collective opinion is far better.

For instance, one self-proclaimed expert appeared on CNBC in 2014 stating that the Dow Jones Industrial Average, one of the most widely watched indexes, would fall from its then current 16,000 level to 6,000 by 2016—a 63% drop. In mid-December 2016, the Dow was approaching 20,000—a 25% increase. That's not even in the right zip code, much less the ballpark. Though I tended to agree with him then, and I still feel financial markets are well overvalued, I have yet to command the up to $70,000 fee for speaking at corporate events that he can.

A popular trading site claims you'll be able to quit your day job and do nothing but make an easy six-figure income from home. The price? A mere $25,000 for about six weeks' worth of information. If it was that easy, these firms wouldn't have that kind of time to spend with you. And they certainly wouldn't want the secret to get out. These firms have instead figured out that there's always someone willing to believe, someone willing to try, and someone willing to part with $25,000.

It's not just the small-time websites where problems occur. One of the more infamous cases was with Long-Term Capital Management (LTCM), a hedge fund formed in 1994 by John W. Meriwether, who was the head of bond trading at Salomon Brothers. Even more impressive, the fund hired not one but two Nobel Laureates in Economic Sciences—Myron S. Scholes and Robert C. Merton—to run the fund. What could go wrong?

Nothing—at least in the beginning. The fund returned 21%, 43%, and 41% in its first three years, impressive numbers that outperformed the overall markets by a long shot. But in the next two years, it faced the Asian financial crisis and the Russian financial crisis and lost $4.6 billion in less than four months. It caused a near worldwide financial meltdown, which required assistance from the Federal Reserve.

That's what can go wrong.

Nobody can control or predict the markets. Nobody can possibly understand all the things that could occur in the future. Yet, when a couple of high-profile experts are put in charge, it's a subconscious assumption that they must know something. Therefore, people think it's a sure-fire bet for financial freedom. They invest heavily—and lose big.

You must always remember that no single person, or even small group of people, can possibly know more than the collective opinion of the world. It never hurts to ask for opinions, but think twice about paying for questions to which nobody can have the answer. You're likely to get expensive bad information—and have no way of knowing it until it's too late.

What about Experts Who Get It Right?

Many "experts" have an aura because they made one seemingly accurate prediction. They milk it for all its worth, write books, and make lots of self-promotions over that one prediction. However, if you look at the history of any expert, you'll find hundreds of other predictions that were far off-base. One correct prediction doesn't make him an expert. It makes him a person who takes many shots at the dartboard and occasionally hits the bullseye.

Mathematically, it's not difficult to show. If you flip a coin 10 times, one person will guess the exact sequence—*if* you have a couple thousand people making guesses. That doesn't mean you should pay that person for advice if you were to toss the coin another 10 times. But if that person writes a book, appears on CNBC, and sends tweets under a flashy Wall Street name, it's hard to convince people that he's not an expert.

Wall Street is filled with pundits, probably millions of people around the world, all making guesses about what the market will do. Under those circumstances, somebody will get it right.

The bigger test, however, is to not focus on the one or two apparently amazing predictions he made. Instead, see how many times he's made predictions and how often he was right. If you take that approach, you'll see he makes hundreds of predictions—most of them wrong. But it's his one right prediction you'll read about on his websites and social media sites and in his new books. In most cases, the "expert" status comes from years of great promotions, not years of great predictions.

For the mystifying world of the stock market, there are always people willing to pay for information they think is going to make them money. But if they understood how markets work and the incentive of profits in the markets, they'd understand that it's impossible for one person to know enough information to predict how people will respond.

As long as people believe these experts exist, however, it ensures many will advertise to be that guru. They'll tell you exactly where the market's going, which sectors will be up, and which will be down. They tell people exactly what they want to hear, and they gather followers. If they sound smart, have impressive backgrounds, and flashy diplomas from Ivy League schools, nobody questions it. And if they call themselves an expert and have a #1 bestselling book, nobody doubts them.

What makes the stock market particularly vulnerable to producing so many of these "experts" is that there's no way to prove they're not what they claim to be. For most professions, you need to be licensed, have an appropriate educational background, or have a certain level of experience. None of that is true for being a stock market expert. Anyone can cast an opinion, and there's no way to tell whether it's good or not.

Today, "expert" and "professional" are overused buzzwords. Anyone can be an expert. You can find expert party planners and expert dog walkers. When it comes to financial planning and investing, it's no different. In fact, in most cases, to be a licensed money manager, all you need to do is file a form with the state. There are no educational or experience requirements. And yet, if you talk to many of these people, they'll tell you with all the conviction and promise they can muster how great they are at returning profits to their clients.

If someone says the market's going to rise over the next year, how can another say it's a bad forecast? If it turns out to be wrong, he'll know all the reasons why and say things like, "Well, nobody knew the Fed was going to raise rates that much," or, "Nobody saw Brexit coming," and give other explanations that apparently excuse the inaccurate predictions. As Laurence J. Peter said, "An economist is an expert who will know tomorrow why the things he predicted yesterday didn't happen today."

Most investing experts are like porn stars of the business world. Would you really take marriage advice from a porn star? If that doesn't sound like a good idea, question if it's worth getting real-world advice from investing professionals and economists.

Remember what Warren Buffett said: "Wall Street is the only place that people ride to in a Rolls Royce to get advice from those who take the subway." Maybe marriage advice from a porn star is actually better than money advice from a money manager after all!

CHAPTER 13

ECONOMICS IS EVERYWHERE

Economics shows we live in a world of scarce resources. The things we'd like to have far exceed the resources—per unit of time—we have to create them. The economists' goal is to figure out how to best use those scarce resources, and when they're used in the most effective way, growth and wealth result.

As you continue to learn more about economics, you'll begin to see markets where you never thought they existed. Markets are everywhere because everything is ultimately a balancing act between supply and demand.

Let's close with a final chapter showing some interesting markets and how you can make better decisions by better understanding the world around you—through the eyes of an economist.

Clipping Coupons

Whether you're looking through the Sunday paper or sorting through junk mail, you'll see coupons offering discounts on everything from small household items to expensive professional services.

I remember going to the grocery with my mom as a kid and her taking out her little coupon organizer. Then she'd write a check to pay for all the groceries after they credited her bill for the glass soda bottles she'd returned. Maybe my boys will look back and recall how their mom used the Target Cartwheel coupon app on her smartphone and paid with her credit card and laugh about all the outdated technology from when they were kids.

Though the method may have changed, the principle behind coupons and discounts is the same. So why do companies offer discounts? The typical explanation is that corporations want to give consumers an incentive to try new products, hoping to get them to switch. That's partly true. But there's more to coupons than that.

In chapter 2, I showed you that most products work on a single-price system, which is sometimes called a *commodity market*. That is, one price is publicized by the seller, and anyone who wishes to buy at that price may do so. The only people who buy, however, are those who feel the product is worth more than the market price. Anyone who feels the product is worth less, or perhaps doesn't have the money to buy, goes without.

By lowering or raising the price, the seller can increase or decrease the amount of sales. That's how price acts as a regulator. But if you think about it, for any goods or services, not all buyers will share the same view of what it's worth.

Just because a case of beer may be priced at $25, for example, doesn't mean all buyers think it is worth that much. Some will think it is worth more; some will value it less. If you're willing to pay $30, you'd consider the $25 price a good deal. The difference between what you pay and what you're willing to pay is called *consumer surplus*. In this example, you'd receive five dollars' worth of consumer surplus. For most things you've purchased, chances are you'd have been willing to pay a little more—possibly a lot more—than the sticker price. Therefore, most buyers receive at least a little consumer surplus for everything bought.

In chapter 2 we also learned that the market price is where the level of supply equals the level of demand. At that price, it maximizes the revenues for the seller. If the market clearing price for a case of beer is $25, then no other price can generate greater revenues for the seller. Rather than charging a single price to all buyers, what if a seller could charge different prices to different people? That's a different story, and revenues would be much greater.

But how can you set multiple prices in a one-price system? With coupons and discounts. For example, let's continue with our $25 case of beer. Obviously, there will be many different views on what it's worth. Some may only be willing to pay $15 or $20, while others may be willing to pay $30 or more. If the seller charges $25, it will only sell to buyers who value the beer at $25 or more. However, if he offers a coupon for $5 off, he can now also sell to all buyers who value the beer at $20—and revenues increase.

But doesn't that mean everyone will now pay $20 and revenues will decrease? This is the trick to coupons. Coupons have a cost. You must search for them, and that means there's an opportunity cost. People with money or little time to clip coupons will just pay the $25 market price. However, buyers with lower valuations may have lower-paying jobs, more time on their hands, or any number of reasons that make it worth their while to search for better deals.

The trick for the seller is to identify which customers are willing to pay the market price and which will only buy with coupons. The beautiful solution is that the coupons automatically do the job. Only those who find it worthwhile will show up with coupons.

When sellers attempt to charge different prices to different people, economists call it *price discrimination*. Don't think of the word *discrimination* in the negative sense in this context. We're not talking race or age discrimination. In this instance, discrimination just means that you can "separate" or "distinguish" between things. That's what the seller is doing with price discrimination.

Price discrimination strategies come in many forms, not just coupons. For example, when movie theaters charge a different price to senior citizens or to college students, it's engaging in price discrimination. It may even offer children under a certain age free entry. This allows the theater to capture ticket sales to the mother and father who otherwise may have felt it wasn't worth the movie if they also had to hire a babysitter. It doesn't cost the theater more to show the movie to these people, but it does end up with more revenues because it entices those who value the movie less to spend money they wouldn't otherwise have spent.

Price discrimination is also partly responsible for the high prices theaters charge for drinks and popcorn. It doesn't make a bit of difference to you if the movie costs you $10 for a ticket and $15 for refreshments, or if you are charged $25 for the ticket and offered free refreshments. In both cases, you get the same thing for $25.

However, it does make a big difference to those who only value the movie at $10. By charging $10 for the ticket and $15 for snacks, higher profits can be captured. As with coupons, there's no need to worry about which people are willing to pay for the refreshments. They'll identify themselves by showing up at the counter and making the purchase.

Another example is with airlines that charge different prices for travelers who don't stay through a weekend, presumably business people who have the money and the inelastic demand. You'll even find price discrimination in something as small as a cup of coffee. Some shops charge one price for coffee but charge extra for cream or sugar. It's simply a way to offer different prices to different people to extract more revenues.

It's often believed that prices must be jacked up in other areas to subsidize those who are paying less through price discrimination strategies. Remember, however, that no seller wants to sell at a price above the market-clearing price, so there's no reason for the seller to raise prices just to use coupons. That would mean lower revenue. The idea is to collect sales from everyone willing to pay the market-clearing price but also get additional revenue from those willing to pay less.

When people hear about price discrimination strategies, they immediately think it's an unfair offshoot of capitalism. Rather than being fair to all buyers, those greedy capitalists must devise tricky schemes to get even more money. Economics shows us it isn't true.

Companies stay in business because they're providing needed goods or services. By using price discrimination, they can cast a wider net and capture more consumers. That translates to greater profits. With greater profits, new businesses are attracted to the market, which ultimately drives prices down.

If you're looking for goods or services, especially higher-priced products, chances are there are Internet coupons available for those willing to hunt them down. Google has opened up a world of possibilities that my coupon-clipping, check-paying, grocery-shopping mother of the past could only have dreamed of.

If you own a business, consider creative price discrimination strategies that allow you to increase your customer base and revenues. As long as the coupon price is greater than your cost, it makes sense to offer it. By understanding the economics of price discrimination, you can decrease your costs—and increase your revenues.

Economics of Winning the Lottery

We've all thought about what we'd do if we hit the jackpot and won the lottery. The lure is so tempting that, no matter what the odds, people are tempted to play. What do economists have to say about winning your state lottery?

Most lotteries require the player to select six numbers from a larger list. For instance, to win the Powerball lottery, you must correctly choose five numbers from 69, then one more number between one and 26. It may not sound that hard, but the odds of doing this correctly are slightly greater than one in 292 million. In other words, choosing the correct six numbers is mathematically the same thing as asking players to choose the winning number from over 292 million. Good luck with that!

To add to the deception, someone always justifies playing by saying, "Someone will win." It's true that someone will most likely win because there are usually far more people playing than there are combinations. The lottery is never surprised when someone wins—but the winner is astounded. The problem with justifying play by saying "someone will win" is that it most likely won't be you.

It gets worse. For all types of investments—or gambles—there's a price that makes the deal fair for the buyer and seller. As I said earlier, this is called the *fair value*. For most state lotteries, the payoff—even though large—is about 99% below fair value. In other words, even though the payoff to the winner is large, it's not nearly large enough compared to the odds you're facing. To put it in perspective, the game of blackjack has a house edge of less than 1%. State lotteries usually have the worst payoffs of any type of gamble—including any casino game—you can find.

You'll often see bumper stickers that say lotteries are a tax for people who are bad at math. Now you know why. Because of the odds, economists are usually puzzled about why people would choose to gamble at all—much less play state lotteries. Considering that people are usually risk averse, it's hard to believe anyone would play a game where they have virtually a 100% chance to lose.

Those who play justify it by claiming that the $1 or $2 cost is a small amount to lose while there's so much to gain, so it makes sense to play. Others have theorized that the dollar represents more than just a chance to win. While waiting for the drawing, hopes, dreams, and possibilities come alive. Maybe it's the adrenaline rush that makes it worthwhile.

If you're going to attempt to beat the odds by playing the lottery, are there tactics you can take to improve your chances? Yes and no.

You can't improve your chances of winning. No matter which numbers you choose, the chances for success remain the same. You can choose a perfectly random set of numbers, but it has the same chance of winning as 1, 2, 3, 4, 5, 6 and bonus number 7. If it seems nearly impossible for that series to ever come up, it shows just how difficult it is to win the lottery. It has the same chance as any set of six numbers you can think of.

Gamblers, however, feel that such a series would never happen, which is called a *clustering illusion.* It seems statistically impossible for these numbers to come up because they're clustered in a well-recognized pattern any third grader could see. That, however, doesn't change the mathematics of which numbers can be drawn.

While you can't improve your chances for winning, you can improve your chances for increasing the payoff if you're lucky enough to win. How? Most players select numbers based on birthdays, anniversaries, and other important dates, so most choose numbers from the calendar: one to 31. That means the numbers above 31 are rarely used. By choosing all your numbers above 31, you'll increase your chances for not matching with another player. So, if you do win, you've increased your chances for a higher payoff since you probably won't be splitting the prize with others.

You should avoid other sequences as well. In most states, the two most commonly selected numbers are 1, 2, 3, 4, 5, 6 and 7, 14, 21, 28, 35, 42 (lucky 7s). If these numbers are ever drawn, the payoff may be one of the lowest in lottery history. Chances are that other series based on mathematical progressions, such as 2, 4, 6, 8, 10, 12, will be common too.

By using economics and understanding how people respond to incentives, you can devise a strategy for playing the lottery: choose all numbers above 31, and don't use obviously mathematical sequences. Again, this won't increase your chances of winning, but it will increase the chance that you won't have to split the prize with anyone else. If you have the same chances of winning, but have a better chance of winning more money, then it's an optimal choice. It's the economist's answer to a market of chance.

People see lotteries as games of chance, but through the eyes of an economist, they're a market for money. The lottery supplies it, and people demand it. Chances are, however, it will remain a market that can be exploited for those who know how to play.

Economics of Reducing Crime

A friend told me a story about a guy traveling through Texas who sent him a photo of a sign dangling from a mom-and-pop gas station door: "This station is guarded three nights a week by an 8-gauge double-barreled shotgun. You pick the night." He thought it was clever and funny, but an economist sees much more: the Law of Diminishing Returns, which we talked about with the farmer and his five bags of grain in chapter 4.

Another way to think about the law is if you put more and more resources at work, the amount you're getting in return gets smaller and smaller. For instance, some fertilizer may be good, a little more may be better, but if you continue adding fertilizer, you're going to reach a point where it's not doing much *additional* good. Going beyond that point is a waste of resources. As a farmer, you want to fertilize your crops just enough to get the desired result, but not go beyond that point.

Crime is no different. You can take some actions to deter crime. If you do a little more, you may prevent more. But if you continue to throw all your resources at deterring crime, you're probably not going to be much more effective. It'll be a waste of resources. The gas station owner used this concept well. If he guards the station three nights per week, that's only 43% of the time, so anyone choosing to rob the store has a 57% chance of success. The odds are in the robber's favor.

Why not guard the store four or more nights per week? Because three is probably enough to get the job done. No robber wants to take a couple of shotgun shells in exchange for a little bit of cash and cold beer. If there's a 43% chance of that happening, it's probably enough to deter all break-ins. Guarding the store more nights per week is a waste of time.

Economists see more to the story too. There's a good chance the sign is a hoax, and nobody guards the store at all. Still, a would-be robber must wonder if it's true and worth the risk. If that does the trick, there's no sense in having three sleepless nights each week. This is exactly why some homeowners put fake security signs or mock camera systems on their doorsteps. It's usually enough to make thieves wonder if it's worth the risk. If a sign or fake camera can get the same results as a full-blown, multi-night-vision camera system, why waste the money?

Of course, the answer is that some burglar may not see it, can't read, or just chooses to call your bluff. You now see why economists say you must accept some crime. No system will deter all crime, so you must figure out just how much is acceptable.

A similar idea is at work when you go through airport security. Sometimes TSA agents make you take out laptops, other times they don't. Sometimes you must open them up, other times you can leave them closed. Belts and shoes may come off, and other times you leave them on. Why the inconsistencies?

It's the same principle at work. If the TSA creates a process where smugglers or terrorists can't be quite sure which protocols will be used, it makes it more difficult to figure out how to get illegal substances through. If shoes, for example, are always required to be removed, then it's obvious they don't want to hide stuff there.

But it's also a case of time is money. Fewer flights can be scheduled if it takes too long to get people through security, and that means less business gets done. But if shoes are only required to come off on random days, at random times, for random flights, then it's just as good as always requiring their removal. It may seem like an unorganized system, but it's the same idea as guarding the gas station three nights per week.

A perfect world is a nice idea, but it also means we'd need unlimited resources to make that happen. It's not possible, so the next best thing is to figure out how much crime is acceptable.

What about murder? You'll hear people say we must eliminate all murders because life has infinite value. I totally agree; life does have infinite value. There's no way I could ever place a value on the life of my family and friends. One of my very best friends growing up was shot and killed in 2013 while buying an iPad advertised on Craigslist. He was a 12-year veteran of the Indiana National Guard, did a tour of duty in Iraq, and had a wife and one-year-old son. It was a terribly tragic event, and I still get teary-eyed every time I hear the Garth Brooks song "Rodeo." We'd listen to it on repeat every day on the way to our summer job roofing houses.

While individuals feel their lives and the lives of their loved ones are infinitely valuable, from an economics perspective, it can't be true. It doesn't make sense that a thousand people must die to save one. By the same token, it doesn't make sense that we must use all our resources to be sure nobody is murdered. We can't convert all our aluminum into cameras to watch every street corner, turn all our people into police officers and guards, use all our copper for bullets, and use all our land to build prisons. To do so means we would have no farmland, hospitals, shelter, or other necessities, and many more will die than are saved from murder.

In a world of limited resources, we can't have it all, and that means we must accept some level of crime, including murder. Can we shift some of those resources into preventing crime? Sure, and now you're thinking like an economist. It may be worthwhile to devote *some* resources, if we're willing to lose those resources' other uses in exchange.

Always remember: it's easy to overlook what you can't see. If a new initiative dedicates more resources to reducing crime, and crime statistics shows that it works, it doesn't mean it was pure gain for society. We lost some resources in that exchange. The proper question isn't whether it worked; it's whether it was worth it to lose the lost resources. This is why some economists may talk about crime reduction but won't talk about crime elimination. Be skeptical whenever you hear someone talk about crime reduction or safety improvement that they say is infallible. It can't be done.

Years ago, a newspaper article quoted a senator who said our military deserves the best tanks money can buy. It sounds like a nice idea, but even the military would object. No matter how good you make a tank, it can always be made better if you're willing to throw more resources—and money—into it. Even if you could get close to building the very best tank conceivable, it would be so expensive the military may end up with only one. Would the army rather send in thousands of tanks that aren't quite perfect or just one that is the best money can buy?

Crime is an unfortunate part of life. As long as we have limited resources, we'll always have to deal with making the difficult choice of just how much crime we should accept. Nothing will ever bring my friend back, and the 50- and 35-year sentences his killers got will never bring justice to his senseless death. I know my life and the lives of every other person who knew him are all better off from the time his presence graced us. Hopefully the tragedy will always serve as a reminder for everyone to be vigilant and that crime doesn't pay.

Economics of Casino ATMs

If you've ever been to Las Vegas, I bet you quickly noticed casinos will do just about anything to get you in the door. Each hotel is bigger than the next, offering free drinks, food, and entertainment to entice you. Casinos know that once you're inside, your money is theirs.

Offering incentives to attract gamblers isn't hard. What's odd is that these casinos charge $10 or $20 to withdraw money from their ATMs. If they work hard to get you in the door, why do they make it so expensive to withdraw money? It seems counterintuitive to their efforts, which leaves gamblers puzzled.

Economists have the answer. In chapter 7, we talked about the idea of comparative advantage, which is the ability of one person or country to produce goods and services at a lower opportunity cost than others. We can use this concept to show how the casinos are simply changing relative values.

Let's say you decide to go gambling and wish to limit the amount of potential losses by only withdrawing $20 from the ATM. However, once you see the $20 ATM fee, you'll realize it's 100% of the total withdrawal—far too costly. Rather than turning away or finding an ATM outside the casino, gamblers now have the incentive to make the transaction cheaper by withdrawing a larger sum of money. If you take out $100, it knocks the cost down to 20%. Withdraw $400 and you're down to 5%. That's much more reasonable.

While you may think you've beaten the system, the casino accomplished exactly what it wanted: it got more money into your hands, which you'll likely lose. Few people will pay $20 to withdraw $20 from an ATM. If the ATM fee was $1, however, gamblers would withdraw smaller amounts. High withdrawal fees incentivize the patrons to make larger withdrawals.

Economist Armen Alchian used this concept to solve a similar economics puzzle. Anyone traveling to northern states in the United States, where oranges are imported, will quickly notice that they have the biggest, brightest, juiciest, and best oranges coming from Florida. But if you go to Florida, the oranges are small and not nearly the same quality. Comparative advantage shows why.

If high-quality oranges are $10 per box and low-quality ones sell for $5 per box, then the high-quality oranges "cost" two boxes of low-quality ones. Remember, economists generally don't see things in dollars, but instead as the amount you're giving up. To buy one box of high-quality oranges means you're giving up two boxes of low-quality ones. That's the economic cost. By the same reasoning, if you buy a low-quality box for $5, you're giving up half of a high-quality box.

Now enter shipping costs. Shipping companies care about the weight, not the quality, of packages. If a $5 shipping charge is assessed per box, then the price of high-quality oranges jumps to $15, while low-quality ones increase to $10 per box. What happens to their relative costs? If both grades of oranges were shipped to my home state of Indiana, residents would see that a high-quality box costs 1.5 low-quality boxes. In Florida, however, the cost was two boxes, but with shipping factored in those same oranges in Indiana becomes 1.5 boxes of low-quality oranges.

Relatively speaking, high-quality oranges would be cheaper in Indiana. If Florida growers are going to ship oranges to Indiana and there's a fixed price to do so, they might as well ship the high-quality ones where their relative costs are cheaper and they can sell more. What happens to the cost of low-quality oranges? Comparative advantage says they must be cheaper in Florida.

In Indiana, after shipping charges, low-quality boxes will cost 0.66 boxes. In Florida, that cost was only one-half of a box, which is cheaper. In other words, Floridians would rather give up one-half of a box of oranges than two-thirds of a box. Low-quality oranges would be comparatively cheaper in Florida. Because of a flat shipping cost, Florida ends up with the low-quality oranges, and my fellow Hoosiers get the high-quality ones. Who would have thought? Well, economists!

Now go back to the casino ATM puzzle. The casino charges a flat $20 "shipping" charge to get money from the ATM. No matter how much you choose to withdraw, it's going to be a flat-rate charge. Which are you most likely to get from the ATM: $20 or $100? You're more likely to request $100 since it is relatively cheaper—exactly why high-quality oranges are cheaper in Indiana.

Understanding comparative advantages provides answers to many economics puzzles. Here's two more for you: Why do you suppose many island nations, Singapore for example, use Mercedes and BMWs for taxis? And why would Disney market its high-priced hotels and resorts in Australia, but not to its own Florida residents?

Once you learn to think like an economist, you'll solve many market puzzles and even come up with a big business idea that lands you a promotion. If powerful economic principles are working in the little ATM tucked away in a dark corner of a Las Vegas casino, they can work anywhere.

Union Wages

In 2016, about 10% of the labor force belonged to a union. Unions are organizations that advocate improved working conditions and increased wages for their members. All you do is sign on the dotted line and you're in—provided you pay the dues, which are, on average, about two hours' pay per month.

You'll typically find unions comprised of carpenters, plumbers, auto workers, steelworkers, and electricians. But you'll also find large unions for service employees, including teachers, postal workers, police, and firefighters. Some of the most recognized unions include the AFL-CIO, Teamsters, and the UAW.

What's not to like? Pay a monthly fee and you're guaranteed to have better working conditions, mandatory time off, and far greater protection than you'll receive from the basic federal laws. Better yet, you'll enjoy roughly 15% higher pay than non-union members in the same profession. This is the speech you'll hear from the union bosses. You'll hear an entirely different one from economists.

By now you should recognize that you can't just increase the price of something, including wages, without any repercussions. Something must give. A union's effectiveness depends largely on the education, skills, and supply of its members. Even though unions say they're most effective for improving the conditions for low-skilled workers, the data says otherwise. United Farm Workers, for example, will have little effect on the overall wages because there are so many unskilled workers willing to do the job. Remember, your wages are ultimately determined by how easily you're replaced. Competition keeps wages low.

However, other unions exist that are more powerful. For example, Milton Friedman cites the American Medical Association (AMA) and Airline Pilots Association (ALPA). While the AMA is not considered a union by definition, it is from an economic view. It's an organization designed to improve the conditions and salaries of its members. It does this through limiting the supply of doctors by simply raising the standards required to be admitted to practice medicine. With fewer doctors available, salaries remain high.

Friedman also posed two key questions: Do these people earn higher wages because of a strong union? Or are they strong unions because the workers are highly paid (and thus highly demanded)? If highly paid workers form a union, they have the money and resources to increase its effectiveness, so both are true. The result is that the most effective unions are those involving highly skilled, highly paid workers.

Like so many economic puzzles, the answer is exactly opposite of what you'd expect. Unintended consequences prevail. Union bosses will tell you they exist to increase the pay and working conditions of the unskilled, low-pay workers. That's true to a small degree, but what are the costs? Raising the wages of its members must come at the cost of reducing employment for others. If you raise the price of labor, there's no question that fewer people will get hired, including doctors, attorneys, and pilots. Unions create fewer jobs.

This is part of the reason why healthcare reforms will struggle to balance supply and demand. By making healthcare more available, we'll have more people visiting doctors and hospitals. But if the AMA limits the supply, there will be an ever-increasing imbalance between those seeking medical attention and those allowed to provide it. Waiting times will continue to grow, which is still an increased cost, just in a different form.

Most people consider attorney fees to be outrageously high, but this is partly due to the American Bar Association (ABA), which regulates the supply of attorneys just as the AMA regulates doctors. If we could allow skilled labor, like a paralegal, to perform some legal functions, it would greatly reduce the cost of attorneys.

Do you really need an attorney to read over your one-year apartment leasing contract for $400, or would a paralegal do just fine for $50? How about a retired attorney who is unlicensed? It's a decision you should be able to make, but the ABA doesn't allow it. In fact, it's serious jail time and fines if a non-attorney gives legal advice—even without pay.

The net result is that union workers, which amount to 10% of the population, gain roughly a 15% jump in pay. But it also means the remaining 90% of the population gets lower pay or no work at all. If you count the missing dollars, it's a net loss to society.

The union bosses' speech about improved working conditions depends on which group you fall into. As Friedman showed, the effect of unions has been to increase the pay of high-paid workers and lower the pay for low-skilled workers. The economic puzzle on the benefits of unions is easily solved once you learn to look where you can't see.

Crowd Control at the Magic Kingdom

Disney is called the "Happiest Place on Earth," but if you've ever stood in lines at the Magic Kingdom during peak tourist season, you'll view it more like the Torture Kingdom. Disney, however, is the undisputed master of crowd control. While waiting in line, they build suspense and excitement by showing the upcoming thrills on monitors. Live entertainers and engaging displays are strategically placed to distract you from the wait.

Of course, Disney can regulate the overall crowds by simply raising or lowering ticket prices at the gate. It even uses price discrimination strategies by offering Florida residents discounts while maintaining full prices for out-of-state visitors.

Once inside, however, Disney would have a hard time assessing fees to regulate the crowds further. It can't charge a high price to discourage people from wandering to the right and a lower fee to encourage others to walk left.

Once you learn to think like an economist, however, you realize all supply and demand problems are about balance. In many business applications, balance is easily accomplished by changing price. But if you can't use price, perhaps there are other ways to create incentives.

As an economist, all you do is understand how people behave and then create the desired incentives. Disney, being the master, has done just that. The company has discovered that when most people meet a fork in the walkway, they'll naturally wander to the right. It has also discovered, with all things being equal, that people tend to wander to the widest paths.

If you're walking through the park, you'll notice that where there are forks in the walkways, the paths to the right are usually narrower than those to the left. By making the left path wider, it creates a psychological incentive for some additional people to wander left. However, if they made the path too wide, they'd get too many people turning left. If too narrow, too many people would go right.

The trick, like most economics problems, is about finding the right amount. By making some of the left paths a bit wider than the right, Disney creates another way to balance the flow of tourists inside the park. If you're near the borders of the park, you may see the opposite effect. To get people to flow toward the center, the path to the right will normally be larger than those to the left.

Could Disney use music and lights too? Next time you're in the Magic Kingdom, think like an economist and you'll see it's not all magic. It's economics in a magical form.

Economics of Sexual Misconduct

In 2007, economist Steven Landsburg wrote a wonderful book titled *More Sex Is Safer Sex*. It's a brilliant topic because it defies the public's intuition. Like this book, upon reading the title, most readers think it's just a catchy title to get your attention, or a play on words. But Landsburg shows it must be mathematically true.

Realizing that the truth is often opposite of what you'd expect isn't a surprising outcome to economists. In fact, it's a wonderful gift. You'll see the world in a new way and make better decisions as a result—even deciding who to date or who to mate with. So, to close a book on why economics is like sex, it only makes sense to show that economists study any type of social behavior—including sex—and try to predict the outcomes based on incentives.

Let's consider the economics of sexually transmitted diseases, or STDs. The common logic says that if you're sexually active, there's a good chance you'll contract STDs. If you get infected, you're now one more number added to the pool, and the probability increases for others to get infected. Therefore, by reducing your encounters, you're keeping diseases from spreading. It's logical and sound, but it's also wrong. How can that be?

People select potential partners from a pool of candidates. But let's say, in the name of safety, a national STD awareness campaign is launched, and the sexually conservative people have fewer encounters. The sexually promiscuous, by their very nature, will not reduce their activities, or at least not to the same degree as the more conservative will. The result is that a larger portion of low-risk people drop from the dating scene. The people left behind are mostly the high-risk ones. So any sexually conservative people who still have encounters will now have dramatically increased chances of catching STDs.

However, if sexually conservative people begin having sex, contrary to the media campaigns, there are better chances to hook up with a non-infected person. Even if conservatives catch a disease, they're less likely to spread it since they don't have as many encounters. But when the promiscuous contract diseases, they spread them quickly. With more conservative people in the dating pool, it reduces the chances for the promiscuous to spread the disease. With fewer sexually conservative people, the randy are left to run rampant.

I know what you're thinking. The logic doesn't sound right. If more sexually conservative people enter the dating pool, there's a lower chance of getting infected?! Sure, if any individual drops from the dating pool, his chances of catching any diseases are now zero. But that's missing the point of the disease *spreading*.

What's good for the individual isn't necessarily good for the group. For example, if you go catch a game at Wrigley Field and someone suggests standing to get a better view, it sounds like a logical idea—until everyone tries it at the same time. Believing what works for an individual must work for the group is called the *fallacy of composition*. It's an argument that sounds true but is illogically constructed.

This is the same idea at work for reducing the spread of STDs. It may be better for one sexually conservative person to exit the dating pool, but if every conservative person exits, it's worse for society and diseases spread faster. By having sexually responsible people stay in the dating pool, the average quantity of people and health of the pool is increased, which is to say, the risk is reduced.

If this is still hard to grasp, consider an economics principle coined the *lemon law*, based on a research paper by economist George Akerlof. It was designed to show that bad equilibriums can result when there is *asymmetry of information*—when the seller has more information than the buyer or vice versa.

Imagine that you're considering selling your car to Honest Abe's Used Cars. It's in immaculate condition, has always been serviced, and has low miles. You feel the car would fetch close to $18,000 if you sold it yourself. Honest Abe, however, says that for this model car, he's willing to pay $10,000. You leave and decide to sell it yourself.

The next day, Frankie the "Flying Ace" comes in with a nearly identical car. Although it looks new, he's been using it for daredevil jumps over local ponds for his YouTube channel. It's never had the oil changed and has been repainted several times. He's hoping to get $2,000 for it. Honest Abe, however, doesn't know how the car has been abused; that's asymmetry of information. Abe instead just sees that it appears to be a good-looking car and takes Frankie's word that it's been serviced regularly and driven gently. He makes the same $10,000 offer, and Frankie is a happy camper.

Because of the asymmetry of information, you received a low-ball offer while Frankie got the deal of a lifetime. If Abe typically offers $10,000 for similar-looking cars, the long-run result is that everyone with junkier cars—lemons—will visit Abe often to sell their used-car inventory. Everyone with quality cars will avoid Abe. In other words, anyone with a car whose value is greater than $10,000 will never sell it to Abe. It's only those who feel their car's value is less than $10,000 who are willing to supply Abe with inventory. The result is that Abe will be loaded with lemon cars, which are those cars whose value is far less than what Abe paid. *That's* Akerlof's lemon law.

It's this principle that's partly responsible for dealerships creating the certified pre-owned market. Here, dealers offer their expertise and go through every inch of the car, replacing anything that needs it, and sometimes offering limited warranties. In exchange, the dealer can ask higher prices because potential buyers know the dealer's knowledge and expertise have now been priced into the car.

Akerlof's lemon law doesn't just apply to the used-car market. It says, in the presence of asymmetrical information, you'll get similar pricing imbalances. There's no way for the market to bid prices down because it's not in possession of the same information as the sellers. That story's not too hard to swallow for people who first hear the parable of Akerlof's lemon law principle. However, it's the same principle at work for our dating story.

For those who are sexually conservative, there's no way to advertise that to the market. And just like Flying Ace, there's no way for the conservatives to identify the sexually reckless. The result is that the market, the dating pool, ends up with potential candidates whose "value" is much less than the average price. In other words, their risk level is higher than average. But when more sexually conservative people enter the dating pool, the average health is increased, which is to say, the risk is decreased.

Of course, you can't carry this argument out indefinitely to where the sexually conservative become reckless. But it is true that if more sexually conservative people began to have a little more sex, STDs wouldn't spread as quickly. Who would have thought? Well . . . economists!

Economics is everywhere. Once you learn to think like an economist, you can certainly use those skills to understand the traditional business uses you're used to hearing about, the ones that make people think economics is boring. But once you realize economics is the means of human existence and survival—just like sex—it makes the concepts easier to understand and a lot more fun. In the world of marketing, they say sex sells. Without economics, there'd be nothing to sell.

Every nation is built on economic principles. Sure, some go about it in different ways, but all are trying to answer the most basic questions of what to produce, how to produce it, and for whom. When you couple that with limited land, labor, capital, and entrepreneurship, you realize we can't have it all, so the questions come down to what's the next best solution.

In 1776, Adam Smith realized that the wealth of nations was dependent on specialization and trade. Nations can produce more when people specialize in tasks, rather than trying to do it all. With more output, people can trade those things and become better off. If another country can produce something cheaper, it pays to trade with that country.

No matter how often this message is shared and no matter how clear the arguments, people think they can get something for nothing. Even after the 2016 election, President Trump has continued to push the "Buy American" campaign. We have shown that there is nothing wrong with buying American, but when you factor in the true cost, it's a bad idea—even though it's easy to convince residents they'll be better off. It gains votes.

As discussed in chapter 7, if any country is better at producing a product or service than another country, it then must be relatively better (or comparatively better), and the two should trade. Both will become better off. The same argument can be made for states. If Wisconsin and California can both produce wine and cheese, but Wisconsin is better at making cheese, it should specialize in that and trade with California for its wine.

Everybody seems to get that argument, but it's exactly the same when comparing one nation to another. If everyone jumps on the "Buy American" campaign, we'll get less of everything, including credit, which only means prices rise. When prices rise, we can buy less and are therefore worse off.

The problem with a political campaign like "Buy American" is that it teaches people, and especially the future generations, that we can have it all. It teaches kids that the government is the master and has the solutions for everything. It removes the incentive to produce. Instead, it creates the incentive for people to produce nothing and look to the government for help.

GOP candidate Dr. Annette Bosworth, who showed the government's "lesson in irony," posted something interesting on Facebook. She said the food stamp program that the US Department of Agriculture administers distributes free meals and food stamps to more than 46 million people every year. Meanwhile, the National Park Service, which the Department of the Interior runs, asks visitors not to feed the animals. Their reason? The animals grow dependent on the handouts and will never learn to take care of themselves. So which is the truth? The government can't have it all, but it's trying to, so it creates laws that are logically inconsistent.

I'm not at all saying that food stamps need to be eliminated, or that other special-needs programs don't have benefits to society. Food stamps are necessary for those in need, but the current program penalizes people for getting jobs. It's a system that forces people never to pick themselves up off the bottom.

In a land of such abundance, it *appears* that everything is possible. Just take from the top and give free handouts to everyone else. But remember, it's easy to overlook the forces you can't see. In doing so, we lose the very thing that got us to the top: our free markets.

People who create these multibillion-dollar companies are providing most of the American jobs. They're making everyone better off and more productive, which in turn creates even more prosperity. From the outside looking in, it's easy to focus on what you can see—the millionaires and billionaires who have it all—and think something is wrong with the system. When you understand economics, however, you'll see the free market is the very reason for our success. It's not a reason to have the government try to make things fair. The biggest concern is that there's a growing momentum to push for a government that provides everything. That's the same thinking that brought every communist country into power.

Let's change the social taboos of sex, money, and economics. Take time to understand basic economics, and teach the children so future generations will receive the same gift we have been given: a higher standard of living than that of previous generations. No matter what economic system any country uses, none can provide everything each citizen wants. There aren't enough resources. By understanding the economics of free markets, we can at least get closer to providing more with less.

Money and sex may be taboo topics, but a little common sense about the world around us goes a long way to our understanding why things are the way they are and what can be done to make things better. Money can't buy love or happiness, but economic markets can at least separate the difference between love and lust.

ABOUT THE AUTHOR

Jonathan M. Lamb is a Millennial entrepreneur, economist, consultant, and visionary leader residing in his hometown of Muncie, Indiana, with his wife and two boys.

He is a graduate of the Miller College of Business at Ball State University in Muncie, Indiana, where he earned bachelor's degrees in economics, risk management, and insurance and was also a four-year letter winner as a hurdler on the Ball State track team. Lamb is part of the first wave of Millennials to join the workforce and went on to pursue a master's and PhD in economics before becoming a commodity trader and entrepreneur.

Lamb spent eight years on a trading floor as a spot electricity trader, where he oversaw a book of business with over $3 billion in assets. He has since started seven small businesses and earned an MBA from North Carolina State University, where he was a McLauchlan Leadership Fellow.

Besides managing a multibillion-dollar trading portfolio, he has worked as a business developer for a commodity hedge fund. As a business owner, he has managed a workforce of over 60 employees, owning a construction company, a childcare franchise, a wholesale distribution company, a plumbing company, and a textile company. He currently runs an economic consulting firm and is the founder and owner of an agriculture and energy technology company.

With simple, commonsense economic principles, Lamb is active in holding our government accountable for fiscal policy and laws that impact not only individuals but also businesses, towns, cities, and all Americans. He works and will continue to work daily to raise awareness that in our ever-expanding global economy, economics is the glue that holds the world together.

MorganJames
Speakers Group

www.TheMorganJamesSpeakersGroup.com

We connect Morgan James published
authors with live and online events
and audiences who will benefit
from their expertise.

Morgan James makes all of our titles available
through the Library for All Charity Organization.

www.LibraryForAll.org